4th gs.

bought in 1942

STORIES OF MY COUNTRY'S
BEGINNINGS

STORIES OF MY COUNTRY'S BEGINNINGS

By

MERLIN M. AMES

Teacher of History
J. Sterling Morton Schools, Cicero, Illinois

JESSE H. AMES

President, State Teachers College
River Falls, Wisconsin

AND

ODILLE OUSLEY

Laboratory School, State Teachers College
Slippery Rock, Pennsylvania

Illustrated by

MARY AND **KEVIN ROYT**

WEBSTER PUBLISHING COMPANY

ST. LOUIS   DALLAS   SAN FRANCISCO

PREFACE

Stories of My Country's Beginnings is the first book
of a series covering the entire field of history as at
present outlined for the great majority of American
elementary schools. The book is what its title sug-
gests. Yet it gives an adequate account of how the
western world was discovered by the men of Europe,
how it was explored and settled, and how a new nation,
the United States of America, came to be. The second
book of the series carries the account on to the present
day. Together these two texts present to eager, interested young Americans, nine to eleven years of age, the
inspiring history of their own country.

It is an inspiring story. It is a part of the heritage of
American children. When properly presented, it has in
it the elements which readily appeal to young readers.
In recognition of this fact most schools introduce the
children of the fourth and fifth grades to a more or less
informal study of American history. No one can doubt
that, with the proper materials at hand, worthwhile
results can be achieved.

In preparing to tell children this story of America,
the authors recognized that, despite time-honored
custom, no truly useful book could be made merely by
"squeezing down" the matter found in the average

eighth-grade text into the compass of a book of proper size for the ten-year-old. They saw that not only must the framework be rebuilt to meet a special need, but also the factual matter usually presented required a careful sifting in order to find, and to make the best use of, those elements which will capture the interest and reach the understanding of the young reader.

It was further recognized by the authors that an acceptable text in history, even for young children, must be something more than a collection of romantic episodes, a series of glorified stories about the past. It is their belief that the solid, enduring elements in the nation's history are at the same time its most fascinating features for old and young alike. They believe that the real story of America can be so told that school children will find delight and profit in it.

The outcome of these decisions is manifest in the table of contents of *Stories of My Country's Beginnings*. It is still more apparent in the body of the text. It is the hope of authors and publisher that both pupil and teacher will find here something new, stimulating, helpful.

—THE AUTHORS

CONTENTS

I. OUR AMERICA AND ITS EARLY PEOPLE

CHAPTER ONE. HOW THE NEW WORLD OF AMERICA WAS FOUND

LEIF THE LUCKY AND HIS SAILORS

Norway is a small country across the ocean in Europe. A thousand years ago the sailors of Norway began making long voyages on the ocean. They called themselves Vikings.

Some of the Vikings sailed away from Norway because they thought that their king was gaining too much power. Others went because they liked adventure. Some of the Vikings hoped to gain wealth in the strange new places they visited.

The sailors from Norway went out on the stormy Atlantic Ocean in long, narrow ships. Really, these were not ships at all, but sturdy boats. When the wind was right the Vikings put up sails. But they were always ready to use their long oars to keep their boats moving forward. The men carried their spears and shields with them in the boats.

The captains of some of the Viking ships turned their boats toward the west and went far out on the ocean. At a great distance from Norway one of them found an island and named it Iceland. Another went still farther to the west and toward America and there found Greenland. Viking families went to these islands to live. If you will look at the map in your geography you can see that these islands are like stepping stones between northern Europe and northern North America.

One Viking went in his ship far to the south and west of Greenland. He and his men saw through the mists a long, wooded shore. They did not land on the strange shore, but went back to the Viking settlements and told about what they had seen.

Leif Ericson's voyage. Leif, the son of Eric the Red, heard about the new lands. He made up his mind to see

them for himself. He took with him thirty-five companions and began his voyage. For a long time Leif and his men saw huge icebergs floating about. In places there were a great many fish. After many days of hard rowing the travelers saw land before them. When they drew near to the shore they saw the mouth of a broad river. They pushed their boat up the winding stream until they came to a small lake. Here the men went on shore and made a camp.

There is a story that one of Leif's men wandered away into the woods and came back with his mouth drawn up as if he were trying to whistle. He had found some half-ripe grapes and was trying to eat them. Leif at once named the new country Vinland.

When Leif's ship made the voyage back to the Viking settlements, it carried a load of fine, straight timbers. Timber was needed in Greenland, for no large trees grew there. Soon other ships came to Vinland to get timber. But after a few years the Vikings lost interest in Vinland. No more ships came to the newly-found land. Soon Vinland was almost forgotten.

Learning about Vinland. For many years the people of England and France and other countries in Europe knew nothing about the adventures of the Vikings. They never even heard of Vinland. But after a while the people in Europe began to travel about and see more of each other. The sailors of many countries met and talked together.

Over and over again the sailors from Norway told stories about the long voyages of the old Vikings. They told about a place called Vinland which the Vikings had found. Slowly the sailors and the wise men of Europe learned that the Vikings had found islands in the western ocean and had made settlements on them. They heard of other lands found by the Viking sailors far across the sea.

Today we know that Leif Ericson's Vinland was our America. But none of the Vikings came to America to make their homes. Vinland was almost forgotten. Our great continent was not much better known than it had been before the sailors from Norway set foot on it. So you see, our America was found a long time ago. But it was lost once more and had to be found all over again.

Match the words in the first list with the phrases that mean the same thing.

1. Vikings   a. sailors from Norway
2. shield   b. a large block of floating ice
3. iceberg   c. the land found by Leif Ericson
4. Vinland   d. a large body of land
5. continent   e. a thing used by the Vikings to pro-
                       tect them from spears or arrows

Why did so many Vikings sail away from their home country?

Why did people almost forget about what the Vikings had done?

The Story of Christopher Columbus

Five hundred years ago there lived in Genoa, Italy, a boy by the name of Christopher Columbus. Christopher's father was a wool comber, or a worker who prepared wool so that it could be used in making cloth. The shop where the wool combing was done was on the first floor of the house where the Columbus family lived.

Christopher knew of places which were far more interesting and pleasant than the dirty, greasy wool-combing shop. One of these was the wharf where the ships came and went. The merchants of Genoa owned many fine ships which came from the eastern shores of the Mediterranean Sea loaded with the silks and cloth and spices of the far eastern lands. Columbus liked to listen to the tales the sailors told about the strange lands and the queer people they had seen. He was sure that the life of a sailor was the most interesting that any one could have.

You need not be surprised that the boy Christopher wanted to sail away into a life of adventure on one of the fine ships of Genoa. Almost every boy living in the busy cities near the Mediterranean Sea felt just as Christopher did.

The older people, too, were interested in the ships and the sailors, even though they never once had set foot on the decks of the vessels. They all gathered at the wharves to watch the ships sail away on their long voyages. They rang the bells and shouted with joy when the ships came home loaded with rich goods from the East.

All the people were proud of their ships and their sailors, and were eager to honor the names of their rich merchants. Is it any wonder, then, that Christopher Columbus liked to watch the great ships come and go? Or that he longed for the time to come when he could sail away to distant lands?

Learning to be a sailor. While Columbus was still a very young man he got his first chance to go as a sailor on one of the ships. Before many years had passed he had gained skill as a sailor. He had traveled about on the Mediterranean Sea and had visited many strange cities in Egypt, western Asia, Africa, and Spain. He had fought in battles against the enemies of Genoa. At last he became the captain of a ship.

But Christopher Columbus was a young man who dreamed of still greater things. He wanted to learn everything there was to know about ships and about strange lands in far-away places. He could steer his ship in a straight course, even when he was out of sight of land. He studied a new globe and map that had been made to show the countries and seas that were then known. He eagerly read a book written by Marco Polo, the most famous traveler of those days. From this book Columbus learned a great deal about the rich cities and the powerful rulers of the East. Slowly a great idea was forming in his brain.

The great plan of Columbus. In the time when Columbus was growing to be a fine sailor, the great merchants were worrying about their trade with the East. The Turks, a warlike people, were making it harder and harder for the merchants to bring their goods safely to the trading cities of Europe. A new, safe way to bring goods from the East was needed. But the Turks were between Europe and the eastern lands. How could the merchants trade with the East without crossing the country of the Turks? Columbus grew certain that he knew the answer to this question.

Now let us suppose that we are at the court of King

Ferdinand and Queen Isabella of Spain. The king and the queen are seated on their thrones. Before them stands a ship captain from Genoa. The two rulers have just been given something new and interesting to think about. The ship captain— it is Columbus, of course—has just made a speech.

"Give me ships and men," he told them, "and I will sail to the west across the Sea of Darkness and will reach the lands where the spices and jewels are found. The world is round, and the East may be reached by sailing west."

This idea about the shape of our earth was not new. Some men in old times had believed this. In Columbus' time many scholars believed the earth to be round, but most people thought it to be flat. King Ferdinand and Queen Isabella may not have been surprised when Columbus told them what he believed. But they were surprised when he told them that he would take ships and prove that the earth is round.

At first the two rulers would not agree to help Colum-

bus make his voyage. But Father Perez, a good monk,
believed in Columbus. He hurried to Queen Isabella and
begged her to give Columbus the ships and sailors he
needed. At last she decided to lend her help to the daring plan of the captain from Genoa.

In a short time three small ships, the "Nina," the
"Pinta," and the "Santa Maria," sailed away across the
Atlantic Ocean. When the land could be seen no more,
the sailors on the tiny ships became frightened. Such
terrible things as they had heard about this Sea of
Darkness! Did not this sea become so hot that it would
set the ships on fire? Would they not come to the very
edge of the world and fall off into space?

Day after day the ships sailed on, and day after day
the sailors became more frightened. Columbus had all
he could do to get his men to sail on with him a little
farther.

The great discovery. At last, on October 12, 1492, the
faith of Columbus was rewarded. He and his men saw
before them low green shores, with palms and other

trees swaying in the wind. They had sailed west, away from Europe, and had found land. It was a great day for Christopher Columbus. He had a still greater day when he returned to Spain a hero.

Look at the picture of Columbus' ships on this page. In what ways were they different from the ships of the Vikings?
What important thought came into Columbus' mind?
What was the most important thing that Columbus did?

Columbus had not reached the land of spices at all. He had found America instead. He had found a part of the same land which Leif Ericson had named Vinland so many years before. He was still thousands of miles from the country about which Marco Polo had written. Slowly the people of Europe began to understand that Columbus had found a great new continent.

Naming the people of America. On the islands and along the shores of the new lands he visited, Columbus found a strange kind of people. They were tall and straight and had coarse black hair and skins of a coppery color. He thought the places he had found were near to India, in Asia, so he named the new race of people Indians. Every time we think about our Indians we are reminded of the odd mistake made by Christopher Columbus. When the great sailor went back to Spain he took some of the Indians with him.

Why we are living in "America" instead of "Columbia." Naming the new race of people was one mistake. Naming the new land itself was mistake number two. Columbus, you see, did not know that he had found a great new continent. For a long time other people did not know it, either.

Then a man named Americus Vespucius crossed the Atlantic Ocean. When he went back to Europe he told about the new land he had seen. He called the place where he had been Novus Mundus (the New World). The idea spread that Americus had found a new continent, and people began calling it Amerige, or Americ's land; and then, after a while, America.

The people did not realize that Americus had seen a part of the very land Columbus had also seen—and had seen first. When they saw their mistake it was too late to change the name. So Christopher Columbus lost the honor of having the New World named for him.

Other bold ship captains. After the time of Columbus many brave ship captains made plans to sail away across the western ocean. One of these was John Cabot, who was captain of an English ship. He steered far to the north and visited the coasts of an island which was named Newfoundland. When he sailed back to Europe he told about the great numbers of fish he had seen near the shores of this island. Soon the fishermen of many countries crossed the ocean each year to fish near Newfoundland.

A Spanish leader, Balboa, went to what we now call Central America, crossed over the land, and saw the great Pacific Ocean lying off to the west. Ferdinand Magellan sailed with five ships to America. He found a narrow, winding strip of water that led him around the southern part of South America to the Pacific Ocean. By this time he had only one ship left. This small ship, the "Victoria," crossed the broad Pacific Ocean, sailed around Africa, and got back safely to Spain.

The "Victoria" and the other ships had started their voyage by sailing west from Spain. Now the "Victoria" came home to Spain from the east. The sailors on the "Victoria" were the first men to go all the way around the world. No one could doubt any longer that our earth is really round.

As the years passed, more and more of the bold, eager men of Europe crossed the ocean to America. Some of them sailed their ships for miles and miles along the coasts of the new continent. Others went ashore and wandered about looking for gold. Not all of them found what they were looking for. But they all saw what a fine, big land America is. They saw its broad rivers and its high mountains. They saw birds and animals and trees and flowers that had not been known to the people of Europe. Wherever the white men went they saw the tall copper-colored Indians.

When the sailors and explorers returned to their homes in Europe, they told about what they had seen and about the adventures they had had. As best they could they drew maps to show what the New World was like. Slowly the people in Europe learned what a wonderful new land had been found. Many of them were eager to leave their old homes, cross the ocean, and build homes for themselves in America.

A. Why did people in Europe think America would be a good place for them to make their homes?

B. How did it happen—
   that the Indians were called Indians?
   that the land Columbus found was named America?

C. Write the missing words on a piece of paper.

The homeland of the Vikings was ____. The Vikings found two islands and named them ____ and ____. Leif Ericson found North America and named it ____. The ships of the Vikings were made to go through the water by means of ____ and ____.

A boy named ____ grew up in the Italian city of ____. The merchants of Italy brought ____ and ____ to Europe from ____.

A king and queen named ____ and ____ gave Christopher Columbus three ships in which to make a voyage. The ships sailed across the ____ Ocean. Columbus thought at first that he had sailed to the shores of ____. He named the strange people he found ____. But Columbus had really found ____.

Many people then believed the earth to be ____ in shape. Columbus believed it to be ____. The sailors on the ship called the ____ proved that Columbus was right in his belief.

D. Is there a large map on the wall of your school room? Find these places on the map:

Iceland   Mediterranean Sea
Central America   Spain
Newfoundland

[14]

CHAPTER TWO. THE INDIANS AND THEIR WILDERNESS HOME

A Road Map of Early Days

Have you ever looked at a road map? Did you notice how many red and black and blue lines cross the map of our country in every direction? Each line shows a road over which we may travel.

Do you suppose that America, when Columbus discovered it, had many roads leading across the land? Or maps to show the roads? Of course not! But there were roads in America before the white men came, and maps also. Not printed maps, of course; "memory maps" would be a good name for them.

Some of the wild animals had roads, or trails, which they always used. The buffaloes had the best and longest trails which they used year after year. These big animals often traveled hundreds of miles. Sometimes they went to warm, sunny valleys where they could eat the grass, even in the winter time. Sometimes their trails led them far up the cool mountain slopes.

When the buffaloes were on the march they went one behind the other, all following some wise old leader.

Year after year the buffaloes went along the same trails. The trails followed the hard, firm ground. They led over the lowest hills and crossed the streams where the water was not deep. But they were narrow little trails often hardly a foot wide; just wide enough to allow the buffalo to plant his broad feet firmly on them.

The buffalo trails did not get any wider, but each year they grew deeper. Years after the white men came, and years after the buffaloes had gone, the narrow, hard-packed buffalo trails could be seen winding far across the prairies.

Indian trails. The Indians were even better trail makers than the buffaloes. They went along the same trails year after year, just as the buffaloes did. Each Indian knew about the trails near his village. He knew all the trails that led to good places to hunt. He knew very well how to follow the trails that would take him to the villages of other Indians.

The red men all had clear ideas about the time it would take to travel to different places. If the Indians were going on a very long journey, lasting many weeks, they said the trip would take so many "moons," or months. If the place they wanted to reach was four days' travel away, the Indians would say it was "three sleeps" distant. That is, they would have to sleep three nights beside the trail before they reached the place.

Often the Indian trails were narrow and winding, much like those of the wild animals. Some trails the

Indians followed when going to make war on an enemy tribe were so dim and so grown with bushes that they could hardly be seen. But near the Indian villages the trails leading to a good place to fish on a near-by river, or those going to places in the woods where the Indian women made maple sugar, were wide and plain. Some of these trails were almost good enough to be called roads.

Use of the Indian trails. When the white men went into the country where the Indians lived, they used the trails made by the Indians. The Indian trails through the woods were better than the white men could make. Later on, when the white settlers made real roads, they often put them right where the moccasins of the red men had once padded softly along. Even the railroad engineers of later times often could find no better place to have the railroad tracks cross a mountain, or follow the bank of a river, than along an old Indian trail.

A few years ago a man who had learned a great deal about the Indians made an Indian "road map." The map shows the great trails followed by the Indians hundreds of years ago. Would this not be an interesting map to see? Perhaps we can all see it some day, for it is kept in one of the buildings of our government, at our capital city, Washington, D. C.

What is the difference between—
1. a buffalo trail and an Indian trail?
2. an Indian trail and an early road?
3. an early road and a highway of today?

A Visit to a Town in Wigwam-land

The white people who came to America to live soon became acquainted with the Indians. They found the red men and their families living together in little villages.

Two of the white men, John White and Thomas Hariot, wanted to learn all they could about the Indians. Often they went along a forest path to visit some Indian village. John White could draw pictures, and Thomas Hariot could write interesting stories of what he saw. The pictures and the stories of these two men were put in a book. This old book gives us a good idea of how some of the Indians lived when the first white men came to America to make their homes.

John White's pictures show that most of the Indian houses in the nearby forest looked like the ones in the picture on page 19. The houses stood close together in a cleared space in the woods. Thomas Hariot said this about the houses: "They are made of small poles made fast at the tops in round form after the manner as is used in many arbories in our gardens in England. In most towns they are covered with bark, in some with mats made of long rushes."

Visiting the Indian village. The white visitors saw fires burning before the houses. Fish, laid on frames of green sticks, were cooking over the fires. The white men saw, a little way on, small fields in which grew corn, pumpkins, and melons. Indian women were at work in these fields. They had to stop working often to scare away flocks of crows and blackbirds. Many of the Indian men were fishing in a small river which ran through the Indian village. Some of the fishermen were trying to spear the fish, while others were spreading their nets in the stream.

Finding other Indian villages. John White and Thomas Hariot lived quite close to the shore of the Atlantic Ocean. They did not dare to wander very far away into the woods. But after a time white men found it safe to follow the Indian trails which led them hundreds of miles away from the seashore. These men found Indian homes and villages which were different from the ones John White and Thomas Hariot told about. Away in the north they found the houses of the Iroquois Indians. These Indians built very long houses, with walls and roofs held in place on a frame of heavy timbers. Many Indian families lived in each long house.

Some white men pushed through the woods until they came to Lake Huron, Lake Michigan, and Lake Superior. Near these lakes they found the Chippewa Indians and their neighbors. The houses of these Indians had rounding tops, and were called wigwams.

The frames for these wigwams were made by pushing the ends of long, slim poles into the ground, and then bending the poles over until the other end of each could be shoved down into the earth. The pole frames were then covered with sheets of bark or with reed mats. Notice the picture of a wigwam on this page.

After a while white men wandered far out on the plains of the West where no trees grew. The Indians living there had no bark or reed mats for the outside of their lodges. Instead they used the skins of buffaloes. But near the mountains the Indians found poles for the

frames of their houses. They set up the poles in a circle, bringing the upper ends to a point. Such Indian houses are often called tepees. At the bottom of page 21 is a picture of a tepee village of these western Indians.

In the dry southwestern parts of our country lived Indians who built their houses along the side of some cliff. The rows of houses were built one row above another, the flat roofs of one row of houses serving as the "front yard" for another row farther up on the side of the rocky slope. Ladders were used by the Indians to get from one "street" up to the next one.

The Indians who lived in these villages, or "pueblos," as they came to be called, were farmers, herdsmen, and weavers. Because they were afraid of the wild Indians of the plains, they lived close together in some high place.

Find the part of the story that will help you understand the meanings of these words—

rushes	wigwam	cliff
long houses	tepee	lodge
herdsmen	pueblo	

Nicholas Perrot was a white man who spent many years traveling about among the Indians. He liked the Indians, and the red men liked him. His first long journey was made in a canoe with his Indian friends. Before the trip began, the Indians made a new canoe. Perrot was interested in watching the red men make it.

Making a canoe. First the Indians with their knives and hatchets cut dry strips of cedar from a fallen tree. These they made into the framework of the new canoe. Then the Indian women lent a hand. They brought great pieces of birch bark which had been stripped from the trees. These the women fitted snugly over the frame of the canoe, cutting away the pieces that were not needed. Then, with bone needles, and using fine roots for thread, they sewed the bark covering firmly to the cedar framework.

All this time some of the Indian women had been busy at a small fire. Now they came with an earthen pot full of pitch from a pine tree. The pitch had been melted at the fire. It was now spread thickly over all the seams and joints in the birch sides and bottom of the canoe. The Indian women put on the pitch to keep the boat from leaking.

Now the canoe was just about finished. But the Indian men wanted to do one more thing. They wanted to decorate the new canoe. Using a kind of paint they knew how to make, they put on the front and back parts of the canoe pictures and signs in blue, red, and yellow. After this was done, and after the paint had become dry, the men slid the new boat carefully into the water.

A canoe voyage. Nicholas Perrot was surprised when he saw that the canoe was so light one man could easily carry it. But when he was invited to step into the canoe, and the Indians got in, too, he was still more surprised to see what a great load the small boat would carry.

Perrot and the Indians all wore soft moccasins. The bottom of the canoe was quite thin, and could have been easily damaged by the heavy soles of shoes or boots. The white man and his red companions sat or knelt in the bottom of the canoe, and just along its center line, for birch canoes tip easily. In their hands the Indians had broad-bladed cedar paddles. Those in the middle and in front dipped their paddles deep, and all together, and sent the canoe skimming over the water. The Indian at the back used his paddle to guide the light boat.

At the end of the first day's journey Nicholas Perrot was treated to another surprise. He thought the Indians would paddle the canoe so close to the shore that he could step out on dry land. But the Indians kept the canoe out in the water. Perrot had to step out on a rock and leap from there to the shore. The red men themselves got out and unloaded the canoe before its bottom had so much as grated on the sand and pebbles along the shore. They knew their canoe would soon begin to leak if they were not very careful. After they had emptied the canoe of the blankets and food, they carried it up out of reach of the waves and set it down carefully on a bed of pine needles.

That night the white man and his companions slept in their blankets about a good fire. The next morning one of the Indians carried the canoe over the rocks and set it down in the water of another stream. Perrot and the others carried the camping outfit. In a few minutes the second day of the canoe voyage had begun.

Nicolas Perrot traveled hundreds and hundreds of miles in the birch-bark canoes of the Indians. After a while he could paddle or guide a canoe almost as well as the Indians themselves.

Can you tell a clear story of the making of a birch-bark canoe?

Draw a picture of a canoe. Make pictures on it as you think the Indians would.

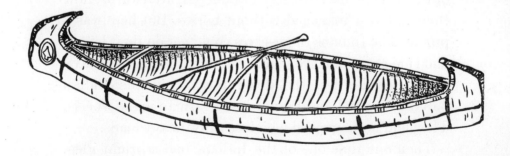

Many of the red people who lived where there were no birch trees could not make birch-bark canoes. But often they wanted to travel on the lakes and streams. These Indians made canoes called dug-outs. Such canoes were really great hollowed-out logs, the hollowing being done with the help of fire. The dug-outs were good and strong, but they were heavy and clumsy.

Many of the tribes of Indians lived so far away from the lakes and deep streams that even a great traveler like Nicholas Perrot never visited them. Going about with these Indians in early times would have been hard work, for they went everywhere on foot. They had to carry on their backs the things they would need on the trip and at the end of the journey. No, that is not quite true; the Indians had dogs, and sometimes the Indian women strapped loads on the dogs' backs when long journeys were to be made.

After a time the Indians had horses. Another story in the book tells about the first Indian horses. The red men of the wide plains must have wondered, afterwards, how they had ever managed without horses. But here was a puzzle. The Indians themselves could get on their horses and ride away like the wind. But what about the heavy robes, the kettles, the dried meat, and the Indian babies? The Indians did not know how to make wheels. They had no wagons in which to draw heavy loads.

Then one time one of the Indians had a bright idea.

First, he found two long, strong poles. He bound the poles together in such a way that the "V" where they came together was above the neck of his horse. The poles rested in a harness on either side of the horse, the two loose ends dragging on the ground behind. With stout buckskin ropes, and with robes and blankets, this Indian then made a hammock, or basket, between the two dragging poles. In this basket were placed the heavy things that were to be taken on the journey. Often the puppies and the Indian babies rode there, too. What a bumpy ride they must have had!

French travelers among the Indians, when they first saw these "Indian wagons," called them by a French name, *travois*. That is the name by which they have ever since been called.

Hunting and Fishing with the Indians

Indian men and boys spent much of their time fishing and hunting. The fishermen had great skill in making spears and hooks with which to catch large fish like the salmon and the lake trout. Sometimes the Indians put log dams across the streams, leaving narrow openings here and there. The fish would crowd close together when they tried to swim through the gaps in one of these dams. The Indians, standing above, could catch them in their nets, or could easily spear them with their stone and copper spears.

The white hunters who first went out on the western plains often watched the Indians hunt buffaloes. Some of the red hunters built two long fences which came together in such a way as to leave a narrow "V" of land between them. Slowly the hunters then drove the buffaloes into this "V." When the huge animals were crowded together it was easy for the Indians to shoot them with arrows.

Some of the Indian hunters put on wolf skins and crept on their hands and knees toward the buffaloes. Since the buffaloes were not much afraid of wolves, the hunters often got very close before the animals became frightened and turned to run away.

Our early America was a land in which there were plenty of fish and wild game. Many of the Indian families made their living by fishing and hunting. The deer, the bear, the moose, the buffalo, and the fish of the lakes and streams gave them food. The skins of animals furnished coverings for the tepees, leggings, moccasins, shirts, bowstrings, and ropes. The animals with fur gave the Indians warm robes for winter, and soft, comfortable beds at night.

The Indian men had to be good hunters and fishermen to keep their families from want. Now and then the fishing was poor and the wild game could not be found. At such times the Indian families suffered from cold and hunger.

Why did the Indian men need to be good hunters and fishermen?

Make a list of the uses the Indians found for the hides of deer and buffaloes.

The white men learned from the Indians how to raise corn and use it for food. List all the ways in which corn has been served to you as food. Green corn would be one, of course. Think of others.

Pretend that you have been on a visit to the Indians. Write a story about "My Week in an Indian Village."

Do you think that traveling on the land or on the water was the easier for the Indian?

How many of you have seen the stone pipes and the stone arrow points and hatchets used by the early Indians? How did the Indians make their stone weapons so sharp?

Tell how the Indians who lived in the woods set up their wigwams.

If you had been an Indian of long ago, would you have wanted to live in the woods, out on the treeless plains, or in the desert? Why?

CHAPTER THREE. AROUND WIGWAM FIRES

FOREST MOTHERS

Indians lived together in families, very much as we
do. And where there is a family the mother is always an
important part of it. How would you like to meet an
Indian mother of the long ago?

Meeting an Indian mother. Here we are, near the low
doorway of a round-topped, bark-covered wigwam. In
the wigwam lives a family of Chippewa Indians, let us
say. Now we see, standing just outside the doorway, the
Chippewa mother. She is wearing a buckskin skirt which
reaches to her toes. On her feet are moccasins, and about
her shoulders a garment much like a shawl. Her small
black eyes look out of a broad brown face. The hair of

this Indian woman is black and straight and coarse. Just now it is drawn into an untidy mop at the back of her head.

The Indian mother keeps her eyes on us, but she says nothing. This should not surprise us, for Indian women do not like to talk when strangers are present. As we look into this woman's face it is hard for us to tell what she is thinking about. Her face is almost like a mask. But that shouldn't surprise us, either, for all Indians take pride in hiding their real feelings from strangers. When the Chippewa woman goes over to a small fire near the wigwam, we notice that she "toes in" a little when she walks. Most Indians did that.

The wigwam-keeper. Indian women worked hard. With the help of the girls, they gathered all the wood for the fires. The women skinned and cleaned the game that was brought in by the hunters. They dressed the skins, tanned them, and cut and sewed all the clothing for the family. The Indian women tended the fields of corn and squash and beans. Of course, they carried the water and took care of the children and cooked all the meals.

The Indian men never helped their wives with the work around the wigwams. They would have felt it a disgrace to help with the work of the squaws. (*Squaw* is a word that means Indian woman.) When an Indian family moved, the women of the forest did all the "packing up" and unpacking, took down the wigwams, and set them up again in the new place.

[32]

Now let us take a peep inside the wigwam. If the day is cold we shall find a small fire in the center of the wigwam. The smoke—part of it—goes out through a hole in the wigwam roof. Our smarting eyes and noses tell us where the rest of the smoke is. We see a number of earthen pots resting on some stones around the fire. Along one wall of the wigwam stands a row of birch-bark baskets, or "mococks." Inside these we might see wild rice, corn, and, perhaps, some smoked meat or fish.

Over at one side of the wigwam we notice a pile of bearskin robes and the hides of wolves and other animals. That, of course, is where the Indian family sleeps. Hanging from the poles that make the frame of the wigwam are strips of buckskin, and what appear to be a few partly-made moccasins. Almost everywhere we look we see something that tells us about the hard work done by the "housekeepers" of wigwam-land.

Perhaps, after all, the Indian mothers of long ago liked the lives they led. We must remember that they had never even dreamed about any other way of living. Of course, they loved their children, just as white mothers do. They taught their daughters how to take care of a wigwam and helped their sons to become brave warriors.

Make a list of the tasks of the Indian women. Which ones are also carried on by your mothers?
Can you find out how the skins of animals were made into soft, comfortable clothing by the Indian women?

Little Warriors

Indian boys had better times than their sisters. Not only the fathers and mothers of the boys, but everyone in the village, was eager to see them grow up to be strong, brave warriors.

Indian boyhood. Small Indian boys played about their homes and did almost as they pleased. They were not asked to do such tasks as carrying water or cutting wood for the campfire. They did not run errands for their mothers. There were almost no errands to run.

But as he grew older the Indian boy began learning the things that would help him to be a useful member of his tribe. If he lived where there were lakes and rivers, one of the first things he learned was how to swim. Almost as soon as he learned to swim he took his first lessons in paddling a canoe. If the Indian boy belonged to an Indian tribe which owned horses, he learned to ride bareback almost as soon as he learned to walk.

Each Indian boy, as you know, had to become a good hunter. Very early in the boy's life his father taught him how to follow the trail of a deer, even when there was only a bent twig or a faint mark in the moss to show which way the animal had gone. The boy hunter spent a great deal of time practicing the calls of the wild animals. He learned to gobble like a wild turkey, hoot like an owl, give the bellow of a moose and the short, quick bark of the red fox. These tricks helped him to creep close to the game he wanted to shoot.

Becoming a warrior. As an Indian boy grew older he went on long trips into the forest. He learned to notice little things, like the thickness of the moss on the north side of a tree. Such things kept him from getting lost in the woods. Quite early he learned how to make bows and arrow shafts. He learned how to fasten the flint arrowheads firmly to the shafts with stout buckskin strings.

Each Indian boy learned from the men of the tribe many stories about old wars and battles. He heard tales of the brave deeds of the chiefs. Sometimes he listened to stories about the gods of the Indians and learned how the gods had often helped his tribe in winning a battle or in finding good hunting grounds.

Each story the boy heard made him more eager, we may be sure, to grow up, that he might show how brave he would be in battle. He was taught to do the things that were supposed to please the gods.

When an Indian boy had grown tall and strong and had learned all that his father knew about the woods and the wild animals, he was ready to be a warrior. If the Indian men thought that he would be brave and true in battle, he was allowed to go to the councils and sit among them. At last the growing boy had become a warrior of his tribe.

What do you think you would have liked best in the life of an Indian boy?

Make a list of the things an Indian boy learned. Begin like this:

1. He learned to shoot straight with bow and arrow.

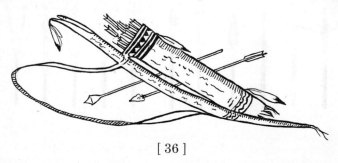

BIG WARRIORS

The Indians did not have kings to rule over them. In each tribe were to be found several chiefs, or head men. Some of these chiefs were leaders in peace. Others led the fighting men when there was a war. But in most things the warriors did about as they pleased. They often gathered in meetings, or councils, to talk over important things.

Indian councils and Indian dances. The Indians liked to go to councils. Often the warriors sat in a great circle, each taking a puff on a great stone pipe that was passed around. Any Indian who felt like making a speech could do so. Some of them could make good speeches. The words of Indians came slowly and seriously. The motions they made with their hands often told more than the words they used.

The Indian men enjoyed dancing. They had many different dances, some of which were the corn dance, the ghost dance, and the war dance. When the men took part in a dance they wore the gayest clothing they had. Their moccasins were decorated with tiny shells or dyed porcupine spines. About their necks they wore strings of bears' claws. Some of them had bracelets on their wrists and rings of copper in their ears. Feathers of eagles and other birds were fastened in their hair. The warriors liked to grease and to paint their bodies and faces in many bright colors. Now and then the squaws had dances of their own.

The Indians and the white men. The white men in our early America saw a great deal of the Indians. Often, at first, the "palefaces" and their copper-hued neighbors lived near each other in peace. After a time the Indians no longer liked the white people.

Sometimes the early white settlers treated the Indians unfairly. The red men began to see, too, that their hunting grounds were being turned into farms by the white people. This, the Indians knew, would spoil the hunting.

All these things made the Indians angry, so they

started to fight with the settlers. After the wars began, most of the white people learned to hate and fear the red men. But there were kind white men in the settlements, and there were good Indians in the wigwam villages. Later stories in the book will tell about some of these fair and just white people and their Indian friends.

Tell what a meeting, or council, of the Indians was like.

The Indians of today enjoy their dancing. Have you ever seen an Indian dance? Tell the class about it.

A Story of Indian Friendship

Many years ago an Indian by the name of Wauwatam lived near the shore of a lake. When he was still a very young man Wauwatam had a queer dream. He dreamed that some day he would take an Englishman to be his brother.

Many years passed by. It was a long time before Wauwatam even saw an Englishman. At last a few Englishmen came to the country of the Indians, but Wauwatam did not see even one that he wanted as a brother.

More years rolled by and then, one day, an English trader came to the fort near Wauwatam's wigwam. The minute the Indian saw this Englishman he knew that this was the man of his early dream. The trader's name was Henry. The white man and the Indian soon became acquainted.

As soon as he dared, Wauwatam told Henry about his

dream. He begged the trader to become his brother.
Henry liked Wauwatam. So the white man and the red
man sat down together and ate green corn and maple
sugar. One after the other they smoked from the same
pipe. In this way the two became brothers according to
the Indian way.

Many Indians lived near the fort of the white men.
They grew angry and got ready to march against it.
Wauwatam feared for the life of his white brother, and
tried to get the trader to go away with him. But Henry
was busy packing his furs and would not go. He did not

think the Indians would start a war against the fort. But the warriors made a sudden rush, leaped into the fort, killed the soldiers, and captured Henry. They made ready to burn the poor trader at the stake.

Wauwatam heard what was going on. He hurried to the great camp of the Chippewas, where Henry was held a prisoner. Wauwatam had in his canoe a large bundle. In the bundle were all the choicest furs Wauwatam had taken in his many years of hunting and trapping. In the eyes of the Indian the furs were worth a fortune, but he did not stop to think about that. His white brother was in great danger. Wauwatam gave all of his precious furs to the great chief of the Chippewas for the freedom of his white brother. So the white man and his red brother paddled away in their canoe in safety.

Read the "Wauwatam" story again. Plan to tell it to someone at home. How shall you begin your story? What shall you tell about next? Plan the entire story before you try to tell it.

AN INDIAN LEGEND

The wise old warriors could tell long and interesting stories about the brave deeds of earlier days. While they talked the young men and boys listened. There was no way to prove that the stories were entirely true, because the Indians could not write down the history of events as they took place. So we must call them legends.

O-kee-wah, an old Indian woman, remembered a

story her father had once told, just as his father had told it to him, so O-kee-wah said. A white man heard the story and wrote it. It is often called "The Legend of the Red Banks."

A very long time ago, O-kee-wah said, the Fox Indians and their friends, the Sacs, lived on a high red bank above the water of a bay where there were many fish. Near the village was a field of corn tended by the squaws. In the woods beyond the corn roamed many deer.

Across the green water of the bay lived another Indian tribe. The men in this tribe wished they had the village of the Sacs and Foxes, where the fishing and the hunting were so good, and where the corn grew so tall and green. They wanted to drive the Sacs and Foxes away and take the village and the field for themselves. But they were afraid to try it alone. So they sent fast runners with the friendship pipe to all the other Indian tribes far and near.

Soon many warriors paddled into the bay in their canoes. Together they joined in a great fight against the warriors at the red banks. The Sacs and the Foxes, with all the women and children and papooses, were hemmed in on the top of their red hill. They could not get away. They could not even get down to the shore of the bay for water. Soon they were hungry and thirsty. But they would not give up. The great fight went on day and night, day and night for many weeks.

One of the young warriors of the Foxes began to fast. He would not eat even the small bits of smoked fish that were his share. For ten days and ten nights he ate nothing. On the tenth night he had a dream. In his dream the warrior saw a tall figure all in white standing before him.

"Fear not," said the strange white being. "Fear not, for when the next night comes I shall cast a deep sleep on all your enemies down below. At midnight they will all lie by their fires as though dead. Go down among them without fear, then, and hurry away to a place of safety." The white figure then vanished.

In the morning the Fox warrior told his friends about his dream. Many shook their heads with doubt as they again crept to the edge of the hill to keep back their enemies.

All that long summer day the battle raged. When night came the tired Foxes and Sacs could see their enemies dancing madly about a great post they had put up in the center of their camp. The dancing Indians were sure of victory on the next day.

But just at midnight the dancing stopped and the dancers dropped to earth and lay still. Soon there was not a sound anywhere. Then the Foxes and the Sacs crept down the hill. The warriors went first, then the women with their babies in their arms and the larger boys and girls clinging to their skirts. What if those sleeping warriors should wake up!

Moving as quietly as they could, and almost holding their breaths, the Foxes and the Sacs crept softly past their sleeping enemies. Not one of them so much as stirred.

When daylight came once more the Indians were in a safe place far away on the bank of a great river. And when their enemies awoke from their strange sleep and hurried up the hill to begin the fight again, not a single Sac or Fox was to be found on the red banks.

This is the story O-kee-wah told to the white stranger.

Could you draw a picture that would help tell the "Legend of the Red Banks"? You could show the canoes drawn up out of the water, the high bank, and the warriors circling about it.

Why is this story called a legend? Do you know any other legends about the Indians?

Find all the "Indian" words in this chapter. Write them carefully in a list.

Find pictures of Indians and of their tools and weapons. Put them in a scrapbook.

Find out what you can about the Indians today. Tell the class what you learn. Are any Indians still living in wigwams or tepees?

Have you ever read about the native people of Africa or Australia? Do they build their houses as the Indians built theirs? Can any of them make boats? Are their boats like the Indian canoes?

Why were the Indians who lived on the western plains glad to get horses?

Why did the Indians need to be good hunters?

Why were the buffaloes and the deer so useful to the red men?

Why did the Indian mothers have so much work to do?

Why did the Indians often become enemies of the white men?

Wouldn't it be fun, now, to make an "Indian" book? You could plan an "Indian" cover for your book. You could put in pictures of Indian homes, boats, and bows and arrows. By looking about, you could find in newspapers or on old calendars pictures of Indians. Some of the best of these could be cut out and pasted in your book. Then you could write in the book many of the interesting things you have learned about the Indians.

II. MAKING HOMES IN THE NEW AMERICA

CHAPTER FOUR. THE SPANISH PEOPLE BUILD HOMES AND START MISSIONS

An Old Town in the Land of Flowers

The hunt for a magic fountain. Hundreds of bold, eager Spaniards crossed the ocean to the new lands Columbus had discovered. Some of them went to South America and to Mexico, often making slaves of the Indians that they found. Here the white men found much gold and silver and carried it away to Spain.

Other Spanish people began making farms where sugar cane could be grown. Still others started ranches and soon had large herds of cattle and sheep. The Spaniards built forts and towns wherever they went in the new lands.

But there was one Spanish leader who was not much interested in any of these things. He was old and he wanted to be young again. His name was Juan Ponce de Leon. He heard about an island, the Island of Bimini.

On this island, so Ponce de Leon heard, there was a fountain. Whoever drank of its waters would be young again. Ponce de Leon wanted to find the fountain, drink some of the water, and again be young. So he gathered his men and his ships and started out to find this wonderful fountain.

Ponce de Leon sailed on until he sighted land. Here he and his men went on shore. It was a beautiful land, where palm trees waved in the sea breezes. The day was Easter Sunday, or Pasqua Florida, in the Spanish tongue. So de Leon named his "island" Florida. "Bimini," or Florida, is not an island at all, as you know, but a long peninsula.

But seek as he might, the old Spaniard could not find the magic fountain. Instead, while on one of his long searches, he received a bad wound from an Indian arrow. At last he left Florida never to return.

An old city. After a time other Spaniards began a town near where Ponce de Leon had begun his search. This town was named St. Augustine. It is the oldest city in the United States.

Many things happened to the little Spanish town in Florida. Once, when England and Spain were at war, an English sea captain landed near by with his men, captured the town, and burned it. Later pirates seized St. Augustine and stole everything of value they could lay their hands on. Then an army from one of England's colonies took the town.

[48]

But armies and pirates and fires together could not destroy all of St. Augustine. Thousands of travelers now visit the little old city each year. They visit the stone gateway built by the Spaniards more than three hundred years ago. One old stone building was once the palace of the Spanish governors. Then there is the strong old fort, San Marco, which, it is said, the Spaniards were a hundred years in building. Now and then the visitors to St. Augustine stop to listen to the deep tones of a church bell. The old Spanish town has heard the tones of this very bell for two hundred fifty years.

Find the part in the story that helps you understand what these words mean.

| pirates | fountain | island |
| forts | peninsula | captured |

A Captive Among the Indians

A Spanish captain named Narvaez decided to explore the coast of the Gulf of Mexico and search for riches. He and three hundred of his men went on shore to begin their search. With them was one of the king's officers, Cabeza de Vaca.

The ships in which Narvaez had reached the land were ordered to sail along the shore and there wait until the leader and his three hundred men came back. The captains of the ships waited for a time, then made a hasty hunt for Narvaez. When they failed to find him, they pulled up the anchors once more and sailed away to the West Indies.

The soldiers of Narvaez were worn and tired when they came out to the shore of the Gulf. They were almost without hope when they did not see the ships which were to take them away. But Narvaez soon set them to work building boats. In these they at last rowed away.

They followed along the shore hoping they could reach the settlements in far-away Mexico. They dared not go far from the shore in their small boats. At last they stopped on a marshy island. Winter came and one night the last boat was blown out to sea in a storm, and

on that boat was the leader, Narvaez. He was never heard of again.

The Spaniards had a hard time of it on their little island. The drinking water was not fit to use. The damp food made the men sick. When spring came only fifteen of them were still alive. De Vaca was one of them.

A white medicine man. Then some Indians came and took the white men away. Instead of killing or injuring the Spaniards, the Indians regarded them as beings with magic powers. They thought the white men could cure their diseases. They liked de Vaca best of all. They called him a medicine man, or Indian doctor.

When sick Indians were brought to the white medicine man, he said prayers over them and then breathed on them. The first sick men got well. De Vaca soon became a great medicine man among the red men. They did not think his prayers helped much. They had much more faith in his breath.

De Vaca wanted to hurry on to see if he could find the towns where Spanish people were living in Mexico. But the Indians wanted to keep him with them. He

was of value to them. He was a medicine man and a slave at the same time.

Five years passed away. De Vaca blew and blew on thousands of sick Indians. At last he was allowed to move slowly along in the direction he wanted to go. Hundreds of Indians followed him. Whenever he came to new tribes of Indians, he had to blow on all the sick warriors.

By this time he had learned many of the tricks of the real Indian medicine men. He dressed in feathers as they did, and wore many charms. His fame spread far and wide, across the plains and beyond the mountains, and always crowds of Indians were waiting for him.

Cabeza's escape from the desert. But de Vaca was eager to get back among white people. He had news for the other Spaniards. He kept hearing from the Indians about seven rich Indian cities, "The Seven Cities of Gold." De Vaca knew the men of Spain would be eager to find these strange cities across the desert. So he wandered on and on toward the west, practicing his magical tricks and trying to heal the sick. At last he came to the shore of the Pacific Ocean. Before him he saw a small Spanish fort.

The Spaniards of the fort saw a wild figure running toward them. They thought it to be some mad Indian. But suddenly the stranger called out to them in Spanish, "Thank God! Thank God!" It was Cabeza de Vaca back among friends after seven years with the Indians.

[52]

1. Why did the men of Narvaez build boats and paddle away along the shore of the Gulf of Mexico?

2. Why did the Indians spare the life of Cabeza de Vaca?

3. Why was Cabeza eager to find the Spaniards in Mexico?

THE SEVEN CITIES OF GOLD

With Cabeza de Vaca on all his wanderings was a huge Negro named Estevan. When the Spaniards heard Cabeza's story about the rich Indian cities, some of them, taking Estevan with them, started to the north to learn what they could about these golden cities.

Estevan's cross. Estevan was sent on ahead of the others. He was told to send back messengers from time to time. Each time he sent a runner he was to give him a cross for a message. If the runner came back with a small cross, no larger than a man's hand, that was to mean to those behind that there was a good chance to find some gold. If there seemed to be a very good chance of finding a great deal of gold, the cross was to be much larger.

You can guess the joy of the Spaniards when, one day, Estevan's tired runner came into camp carrying a cross that almost crushed him to the ground.

This was the news the Spaniards wanted. They hurried back to the Spanish settlements and gathered a great number of soldiers and horses and pack mules. One of the Spanish governors in Mexico, Coronado, took command of the party and marched northward to find the Seven Cities.

Coronado's march. But Coronado hunted in vain. There were no Seven Cities of Gold in all the wild land. The Spaniards climbed over high mountains and crossed burning deserts. They suffered from hunger and from thirst. They marched hundreds and hundreds of miles

through the lands that now make up the southwestern part of our country. But they could find only poor Indians living in their mud huts on the plains and in their cliff houses among the mountains.

One of Coronado's captains made a great discovery. He and his men came out one day on the very edge of the Grand Canyon of the Colorado River. They stared down into its awful depths and then went on. They were

hunting for gold, and they were not much interested in this wonderful canyon in the mountains.

After two disappointing years Coronado gave up. He led those that were left of his hungry and ragged followers back to the settlements in Mexico. It was a long time before the Spaniards built forts and towns in the country Coronado had explored in his search for gold.

Prepare to tell this story to another class. First, make a list of the things you want to mention. You might start with this: The news brought by Cabeza de Vaca.

Taming Wild Horses

Coronado and his men hunted on horseback for the Seven Cities of Gold. Wherever they went the Indians gazed on them with wonder. They had never before seen "palefaces." They wondered at the shining steel armor of the white warriors. Never before had they seen such keen, shining knives and swords as those carried by the strangers. And when the guns of the Spaniards roared, the red people fled in terror.

But the thing that surprised them most of all was the great, four-footed beasts that bore the Spanish soldiers wherever they wanted to go. None of the Indians had ever before seen a horse. Perhaps they even thought, at first, that horse and man were one.

After Coronado had given up his search and marched away to the south, the Indians made a discovery. In the mountain valleys they found animals just like those the Spaniards had ridden. Some of the horses of Coronado or of other Spaniards had run away and had begun to wander about where they pleased. They had almost become wild horses. When young colts were born they grew up without ever knowing what it was to have a master. These were true wild horses.

Some of the Indians must have remembered how the white men had ridden rapidly about on the backs of their horses. The idea came to these Indians that if the white strangers could stick on the backs of these ani-

mals, they could do it, too. Very patiently they went to work, and after a while succeeded in capturing some of the wild horses. Then, after many bad falls, no doubt, they learned to ride them.

How happy the Indians of the great plains were to have horses. Now they could easily hunt the buffaloes and the deer. When they got ready to move their tepees, the horses could carry the heavy loads on their backs, or drag them behind on the travois. If the places where drinking water was to be had were many miles apart, the Indians no longer had to worry about it. On horseback they could travel great distances in a few hours.

Indian warriors living farther to the north heard about the wonderful animals owned by the Indians near to Mexico. They were willing to trade almost anything they had for a horse. Not many years passed before most of the Indian tribes in all the western country owned herds of fine strong little horses.

How would you train a horse to let you ride on his back?

Why were the western Indians eager to tame the wild horses they found?

Match the words with the phrases that mean the same thing:

1. travois   a. steel covering worn by soldiers
2. palefaces   b. a young horse
3. armor   c. white people
4. colt   d. platform on poles pulled by horse

The Spaniards in northern Mexico became interested in a great river which they had found. They named it the Rio Grande. When they marched upstream along the bank of this river they found themselves in a new and strange country. They decided to make a settlement on the bank of the river. Soon a company of Spanish soldiers and a band of friars, or religious brothers, began laying out a town. They named it Santa Fe. They built there a fort and a church.

Many Indians lived near the new Spanish town. The land was dry, but the Indians raised crops of corn on small fields where the soil was kept moist by means of small ditches. The ditches led streams of water from

the river to the fields. The Indians were skilled at making earthen pots, baskets, and blankets. Their houses, set close together and one above the other, were made of sun-dried clay.

The Indians had strange religious customs. The Spanish friars worked hard to get the Indians to become Christians. Soon there were ninety Indian villages in which the Christian church service was carried on.

But many of the Indians did not like the friars. They liked the Spanish soldiers still less. The Spaniards were often unkind in dealing with the simple red men. The Indians were even made to pay a tax to support the Spanish soldiers.

At last a chief named Popé decided that things had gone far enough. He talked with the other chiefs, and they all agreed to turn on the white strangers and try to drive them away. Popé then gathered a great many pieces of rope. In each piece of rope he tied ten knots. Then he sent a fast runner with one of the ropes to each chief of a village up and down the country.

"Untie one knot in your rope each day," began Popé's message to the chiefs. "When the last knot is untied, that is the day we rise against the white men."

The chiefs got quite close to the last knot. Then the Spanish soldiers learned what was going on, and the march, when it came, was no surprise to them.

When an army of the Indians came close to Santa Fe, they saw that the white people were ready for them. So they stopped and sent a messenger to the town with two crosses. One was white; the other red. The Indians agreed that if the Spaniards chose the white cross, they would go away without a battle. But if the Spaniards chose the red cross, that meant war. The white men chose the red cross and there was a great battle.

Many Indians and a number of the white men lost their lives in the war around Santa Fe. The white people were driven away from many of the Indian villages. When the war ended, the friars were able to go back to their work of making Christians of the red men.

One thing they noticed in all the villages: though the angry warriors had burned the churches and killed the friars, they had put safely away all the sacred vessels and signs of the Christian Church. This made the friars feel sure that the Indians, in spite of all that had happened, were really touched by the message of Christianity.

A. Write the words that would complete these sentences:
1. The Spaniards found a great, new river and named it ____.
2. The Indians living near the river had skill at making ____.
3. The white men helped the Indians by ____.
4. But they harmed them by ____.

B. Tell how the chief Popé made his "knotted rope" calendar.

Father Serra's Vision

When the Spanish leaders in Mexico heard about California, they wanted to add its rich lands to Spain's possessions. The Spanish friars were eager to go to California to try to win the Indians to the Christian Church. The leader of the friars was Father Serra.

At last the Spaniards marched north toward California. In the long line of marchers were soldiers and Indians from Mexico. Hundreds of pack mules carried great bundles on their backs. Eagerly traveling to the north with the soldiers was Father Serra.

The good father stopped, at last, and built a bark church. Above it towered a tall wooden cross. Father Serra began to preach to the Indians who lived near.

At first the Indians did not like the Spaniards. They began a war, killed some of the white people, and destroyed the church. The Spanish soldiers wanted to punish the Indians, but Father Serra would not let them.

In a short time a new and fine church was built at San Diego. The friar worked as hard as anyone at laying up the heavy stones for the walls.

But the Spanish soldiers wished to return to Mexico. Their food was almost gone. Father Serra was troubled, for he feared his church would fail if the other Spaniards did not stay to help him. But he made up his mind to stay, no matter what happened.

A ship bringing fresh supplies from Mexico had been promised. Father Serra knew the coming of the ship would make the men feel more contented. But the days passed and no ship came. Father Serra began to pray to God to hasten the ship forward. Then, one day, looking out across the water to the south, he and the soldiers saw, as plain as could be, the masts and hull of a ship. The relief ship at last! The soldiers, who were about to march away, promised to remain. Father Serra was happy.

But still the ship did not come. The white men could not even see it any more. The days passed, three of them, and still there was no ship. But on the fourth day the relief ship sailed into the harbor at San Diego. Where had the ship been those four long days? The captain said that, four days earlier, his vessel had been many miles away on the ocean. Then how could Father Serra have seen it?

Father Serra believed he knew the answer. He believed God had made the soldiers see the ship so that they would wait a few more days. This had happened on the nineteenth day of the month. All the rest of his life, Father Serra held high mass on the nineteenth of every month in the year.

As the years passed, the Church Fathers succeeded in building many fine churches up and down the beautiful California valleys, and in other parts of what is now the southwestern part of our country.

Can you make good sentences out of these beginnings?

1. The city of St. Augustine is ____.
2. Cabeza de Vaca told the other Spaniards about ____.
3. Ponce de Leon hunted in Florida for ____.
4. Father Serra went to live among the Indians because ____.
5. When they reached the Colorado River, Coronado's men found ____.

6. The Indians believed that Cabeza de Vaca could ____.

7. Some of the Indians discovered that Coronado had left behind ____.

8. On the Rio Grande the Spaniards began a town called ____.

9. The friars were sure that the Indians liked the Christian religion, because ____.

Find a picture of an old Spanish church in California or some other southwestern state.

Try to draw a picture of an Indian on horseback. Put a long feather in the Indian's hair, and a long spear in his hand.

CHAPTER FIVE. STORIES ABOUT THE FIRST ENGLISH SETTLERS

SIR WALTER RALEIGH AND HIS LOST COLONY

Sir Walter Raleigh was one of the leading men of England. He had a great deal of money and many friends. Even the queen of England, Elizabeth, gave him her friendship. She was called the "virgin queen" because she had never married.

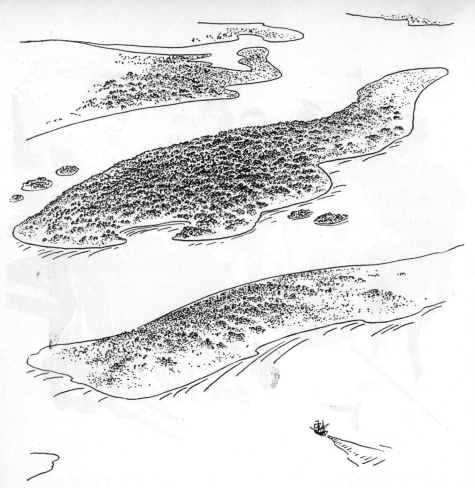

Sir Walter believed that his country should send
English settlers to the new land of America to make
their homes. Queen Elizabeth told him he might start
a colony across the sea. The first thing Raleigh did was
to send men in a ship to find a good place for his colony.

When these men came back to England they told
Raleigh they had found a pleasant island near the coast
of America. The soil on the island was good, they said,

and the climate mild. The island was called Roanoke Island.

Sir Walter Raleigh was pleased with the news his sailors brought to him. He told Queen Elizabeth about his plan to start a colony on the island.

"As I am called the virgin queen," said she, "I will name all of that new country beyond the sea Virginia, after myself." That is how our state of Virginia got its name.

The first settlers that Raleigh sent to Roanoke Island did not stay there very long. They did not like being away from their friends. When an English ship came to the island they were glad to leave their new home and sail back to England. Raleigh was disappointed, but he did not give up. Instead, he sent out a still larger band of settlers, or colonists. Some of the colonists were women.

Virginia Dare. This new group of settlers also built their fort and their houses on Roanoke Island. John White was their governor, or leader. The daughter of John White was married to a man named Dare. On August 18, 1587, a baby girl was born in the Dare cabin. Her parents named her Virginia. Virginia was the first English child born in America.

Roanoke Island was a good place for the new town. The days were warm and sunny. Large trees shaded the log houses. The soil was good for crops of grain and vegetables.

Indians lived on the island and on the nearby shores of Virginia. Although they acted friendly enough toward the white people, they were really not at all pleased to have John White and his settlers on the island. Raleigh's first colonists had burned some of the Indian corn fields because one of the Indians had stolen a small cup. This act of the first settlers had turned the Indians against all white people. They wanted to punish John White's colonists for the earlier wrong they had suffered. Indians remember for a long time any injury done to them. But the Indians on Roanoke Island hid their real feelings so well that the white people believed their red neighbors to be friendly.

Croatoan. Now John White had to go back to England to get more supplies for his colony. When he was ready to return to the island there was no ship to take him. England and Spain were at war, and it was not safe for English ships to try to cross the ocean to America.

For three years the anxious leader waited for a chance to go back to Roanoke Island. At last an English captain sailed in his ship for the shores of North America. John White was a passenger on the vessel.

After a long voyage the ship drew near to the low green shores of Roanoke Island. On the ship's deck stood a trumpeter. John White stood beside him and told him what calls to give on his trumpet. These were the signals the people on the island had been told to listen for. The trumpet sounded again and again. But there were no answering calls from the shore. Not a person was to be seen.

John White, filled with anxious fears, stepped on shore. Only ruins were to be seen where the fort and the houses had once stood. Wild vines covered the ruins. Deer sprang through the openings between the partly burned logs and bounded away. Scattered about in the bushes were a few rags, bits of furniture, and broken dishes.

Then the heavy-hearted leader found something. On a tree were cut the letters of a single word, "Croatoan."

Croatoan was a place where friendly Indians were supposed to live. Had the settlers gone away to Croatoan? John White thought so. He believed the message on the tree told him to go to Croatoan to find his lost people.

But the captain of the ship and his sailors were anxious to sail away. They would not give the leader time to make the search. Sadly he returned to England on the ship. Other men later hunted for the lost colonists, but they were never found. No one knows what happened to them. John White never again saw his daughter and his little grandchild, Virginia Dare.

Find the part of the story which helps you understand who or what these were:

Roanoke Island   Croatoan

The Virgin Queen   John White

Virginia Dare

THE VIRGINIA SETTLERS AND THE INDIAN PRINCESS

One spring day three English ships sailed into a broad bay on the shore of Virginia. On the ships were more than a hundred men. They had been sent to make a settlement in America.

A wide, deep river flowed into the bay. The ships sailed up the stream until the leaders on the ships found a place to stop and begin building a village. The men named the river the James River after King James I, who was then King of England. They called their new town Jamestown.

All the men on the ships were tired of the long sea voyage from England to America. The sunny open

places, the green grass, and the fine trees all about their new home made the men glad that the long journey was at an end. One of the men wrote about what he saw. He said, "The faire meddowes and goodly tall Trees, with such fresh-waters runninge through the woods as I was almost ravished [overcome] at the first sight thereof." Perhaps you will not like this man's spelling very well, but you will understand how happy he was to be in Virginia. Later on he saw something else that pleased him. He wrote, "We came into a plot of fine and beautiful strawberries, foure times bigger and better than ours in England."

Captain John Smith. The men at Jamestown soon forgot their first happiness. Many of them did not know how to do the rough, hard work needed in building forts and houses in the woods. Some of them were lazy and would not even try. Captain John Smith, one of the leaders, made a rule that said, "Those who will not work shall not eat." After that all the men worked better.

After a few weeks numbers of the men became ill. Soon there were more sick and dying men than there were well ones. The food that had been brought from England in the ships began to give out. What was left was not fit to eat.

Captain Smith saw that something would have to be done. He took a few men with him in a boat and started away to visit the Indian villages. He thought he could trade cheap manufactured goods for some of the corn and beans raised by the Indians.

Pocahontas. Strong tribes of Indians lived in Virginia. The red men did not feel very friendly toward the white strangers. Their great chief, Powhatan, ruled over them like a king. Powhatan was fond of his young daughter, Pocahontas.

Captain Smith had many thrilling times as he wandered about among the Indian villages gathering food for his hungry men in Jamestown. At one time Powhatan held Smith a prisoner, and got ready to put the white man to death. Smith's life was spared, so he afterwards said, because Pocahontas begged her father to let the prisoner go.

A short time later, Captain Argall, one of the Englishmen, became angry at Powhatan and his warriors. He thought of a way to get even for the things the Indians had done to some of his men. He took a boat and went up the river to a place near the village of the chief. Then he showed a shiny copper kettle to a poor

Indian and his wife. They wanted the kettle more than
they had ever wanted anything in their lives. Captain
Argall made them understand how they could earn the
kettle.

Little Pocahontas came down to the river to see the
white men's boat. The Indian and his wife begged her
to climb into the boat with them. Then they slipped
away with their kettle, and the Indian girl was left, a

prisoner, in Captain Argall's hands. He took her to Jamestown.

Old Powhatan was very angry. He thought about starting a real war with the white men. But Pocahontas did not at all mind living in the white men's village. She liked the "palefaces" and they liked her. One young Englishman liked her so well that he asked her to marry him.

The wedding took place at Jamestown. By this time Powhatan was almost over his anger. He sent Pocahontas' uncle to visit the white men and to be present at the wedding. The Indian princess was given a new name. From that time on she was called Lady Rebecca.

After a few years good times came to the white settlers in Virginia. Large farms were cleared along the banks of the rivers. The farmers raised tobacco and sold it at a good price in England.

A. Match the words with the sentences that tell about them.

1. Pocahontas   a. He was an Indian chief.
2. John Smith   b. He made an Indian girl his prisoner.
3. Powhatan   c. He traded cheap goods to the Indians for corn.
4. Captain Argall   d. She was called Lady Rebecca.

B. Why did so many of the Jamestown settlers get sick and die during the early years in America?

A small ship called the "Mayflower" sailed toward the New World from England in the year 1620. At that time only a few white people were living in what is now our country. America was still a wild, rough land.

But the people on the "Mayflower" wanted to make homes for themselves in the new land. They were glad to leave their home country, England. They had not been treated kindly in England because their religion was different from that of most of the English people. They wanted to live in a place where they could go to their own church without being punished for it. In America, they believed, no one would care what church they attended.

The people on the "Mayflower" were the Pilgrims. They had a stormy voyage across the ocean. The ship was so small that the Pilgrims were crowded together in a gloomy place below the deck of the vessel. The people had with them their small trunks, rolls of bedding, bags of seeds they hoped to plant in the soil near their new homes, spinning wheels, tools, and guns. The most precious thing each family had was a Bible. The Pilgrims hardly had room to turn around in the damp, dark place where they had to stay.

It was almost winter time when the "Mayflower" brought the Pilgrims to America. Storms drove the small ship out of its course. When the Pilgrims at last

saw land, they were disappointed because it looked cold
and snow lay on the ground. They had hoped to make
their new homes where the weather was warm and pleasant. But they made up their minds to build their settlement somewhere on the stormy shore before them.
The "Mayflower" came to anchor near the tip of what is
now called Cape Cod.

Before the Pilgrims went on shore to find a good place for their town, the men all gathered in the cabin of the "Mayflower." Spread out on a table was a written paper. One by one the men signed the paper. The paper said that all who signed it agreed to obey the laws and rules made by the officers they elected to govern them. In this way the Pilgrims made a plan for governing themselves even before they began building their town.

In this story these sentences are used:

1. "The most precious thing each family had was a Bible."
2. "Storms drove the ship out of its course."
3. "The 'Mayflower' came to anchor."

What does each mean?

Cape Cod, where the Pilgrims first landed, was a sandy place where the wind blew a great deal. The Pilgrims did not want to build their town on Cape Cod. They wanted to find a place where the soil was rich, and where there were large trees. They thought it would be pleasant to have a clear stream flowing through the land where they built their homes and made their farms.

Bands of Pilgrims began hunting here and there for a good place to make a settlement. On these journeys the men carried their heavy guns. Some of them wore armor to shield them from the arrows or spears of the Indians.

Miles Standish was always the leader. He was a soldier. He was brave, but careful. He tried to guard the men with him from sudden dangers. Whenever the Pilgrims had to go through the woods Miles Standish always marched in front.

One day eighteen of the men started away from the
"Mayflower" in a large boat. Miles Standish was with
them. They made a long search for a place to build the
Pilgrim town. Once a storm drove the boat to the rocky
shore of an island, where it was almost smashed in
pieces. At another time, when the Pilgrims were looking
about on the land, a band of Indians swarmed about
them and tried to drive them away.

At last Miles Standish and his companions found a
place that suited them. The land sloped up from a safe
harbor. A part of the ground had been cleared, but
near by still stood many fine, large trees. A clear stream
crossed the land and emptied its waters into the bay.

Then the leader and his men returned to the "Mayflower." The women and children and the other men waiting there were pleased over the news brought to them by Standish. They were tired of living cooped up on the ship.

The anchor of the "Mayflower" was soon drawn up, and the ship sailed across the water to the small harbor the men had found. All the Pilgrims hurried to the shore. They wanted to see the place where their new town was to be built.

The town-that-was-to-be received the name of Plymouth. A large rock where, it is said, the first of the Pilgrims set foot on the new land, has ever since been called Plymouth Rock. A fine monument stands there today.

In their new home the Pilgrims were surrounded by many dangers. They were glad that Miles Standish, their brave soldier, was always at hand to help them meet these dangers.

Finish these "because" sentences.
The Pilgrims left England because ＿＿＿.
They did not want to build homes on Cape Cod because ＿＿＿.
It was dangerous to go through the woods because ＿＿＿.
They built a settlement at Plymouth because ＿＿＿.

Squanto, the Good Indian

How hard the Pilgrims worked to build their new town of Plymouth! One of the men wrote down the things that happened each day. Once he wrote:

"Saturday, the three-and-twentieth, so many of us as could went on shore, felled and carried timber to provide themselves with stuff for building." Farther on he wrote: "Monday, the five-and-twentieth, we went on shore, some to fell timber, some to saw, . . . and some to carry, so no man rested all that day."

First the Pilgrims built a fort and several log houses. As soon as a few houses were finished, the people left the "Mayflower" for the last time and moved into the new Plymouth houses. Two or three families lived in each house. So many persons were in each house that they had to sleep close together on the floor.

"Welcome, Englishmen!" Indians had once lived

where the new Pilgrim village stood. It was they who had cleared away some of the forest. But a disease had spread among the wigwams, taking the lives of many of the Indians. Those who had not died had moved away.

Miles Standish knew there were many Indians living at some distance from Plymouth. Fearing these Indians might come to fight the people at Plymouth, he kept a careful watch for them. Standish had learned that some white fishermen had once treated these Indians badly, and he thought the red warriors might want to get even with the white people.

One spring morning the Pilgrims were frightened to see a tall Indian come walking down the rough little street of Plymouth. He held one hand high, palm out, to show that he came as a friend. In a deep, odd voice he cried, "Welcome, Englishmen!" The people were surprised enough to see the red man walking toward them. They were even more surprised to hear him speak to them in their own tongue.

In a few minutes the Pilgrims were all gathered around their visitor. He told them his name was Samoset. He made the white people understand that he had learned the few English words he knew from the fishermen who visited the coast.

The settlers were glad to learn that not all the Indians were their enemies. When Samoset went away he promised to send to Plymouth an Indian who could speak English much better than he could.

The red friend of the Pilgrims. Not long after Samoset's visit another Indian came to Plymouth. The second Indian's name was Squanto. Squanto, so the Pilgrims learned, had been carried away by the captain of one of the fishing ships. But this had turned out to be a piece of good luck for Squanto. It was while he was far away that the great sickness had visited the land. When Squanto returned to his village he found that all his friends were dead.

Squanto soon made friends with the Pilgrims. The white people learned to trust him. He taught them many things about the woods and the wild animals, and about the other Indians. He told them to plant their corn "when the leaves of the oaks are as big as a squirrel's ear." He showed them how to bury a dead fish in each hill of corn to make the stalks grow tall and strong. Squanto was a kind, gentle Indian. He helped to make Plymouth a happy little town. To the end of his days this good Indian made his home among the Pilgrims.

Tell father and mother, or someone else at home, about "The Pilgrims and Their Indian Neighbors."

HOW ROGER WILLIAMS BEGAN A NEW TOWN

Roger Williams was a preacher. On Sundays he preached to some of the people who made their homes near where the great city of Boston is today. Many of the people who lived in or near Boston were much like the Pilgrims. They had left England because they wanted to be free to carry on church matters as they chose. They called themselves Puritans. Their greatest leader was John Winthrop.

When Roger Williams stood up in his pulpit to preach he often said things that did not please some of the other Puritans. He said that each person ought to be allowed to do as he pleased about going to church. This angered the Puritan leaders. Then he told the people that the Indians were the real owners of all the land. He said the only fair way for the white people to get it was to buy it from the red men. These words of Roger Williams made the leaders almost as angry as his idea about going to church.

A winter in a wigwam. "That man has windmills in his head!" cried one angry Puritan. The Puritans tried to send Williams back to England. But he ran away into the woods and traveled to the south until he came to an Indian village.

It was winter time, and the preacher was cold and hungry. The Indians fed him and allowed him to live in one of their wigwams. The chief was much pleased when he found that his guest could speak the Indian language. The white man spent the winter with his new friends.

The beginnings of Rhode Island. Some of Roger Williams' white friends joined him at the Indian village. They made up their minds to start a new settlement. The chief liked Williams so well that he allowed him to select a piece of land in the hunting grounds of the Indian tribe. So the white men paddled away in a boat and at last came to good farming lands on the shore of a bay.

It was a good place for a town. The preacher and his friends went on shore and began to cut down timbers for the first buildings. Roger Williams named his new town Providence, because he believed Providence, or God, had watched over him in his troubles.

A number of people in the new towns of America liked the ideas of Roger Williams about church matters. They wanted to go to church where they pleased. Many of these people moved to Providence, or started new towns near by. They got along together without quarreling about their churches. The towns on the fine bay grew into the small state of Rhode Island.

A. Finish these "because" sentences.

1. Some of the Puritans were angry with Roger Williams because ____.
2. He ran away to the Indians because ____.
3. The Indian chief liked Williams because ____.

B. A number of our stories have had something to say about the Indians. Now that you have read them, do you think the Indians really wanted to be friends with the first white people in America? When the red men were not friendly, did they often have a good reason? You and your classmates can have quite a debate about these matters.

C. On a sheet of paper write the words to complete the sentences.

1. The man who kept the early Virginians from starving was ____.
2. Two Indian friends of the Pilgrims were ____ and ____.
3. ____ began a new town in Rhode Island called ____.
4. The word "Croatoan" was cut into the bark of a tree at ____. It was a message for ____.
5. A brave soldier at Plymouth was ____.
6. The ship ____ brought the ____ across the ocean from ____ to ____.
7. Not many Indians lived near Plymouth because ____.
8. ____ was the chief of the Indians in Virginia. The name of his daughter was ____.
9. Roger Williams believed that ____.
10. The Indians were kind to ____, and to ____; but they were not so friendly to ____.

D. Which is the right ending?

Ships like the "Mayflower" crossed the ocean by means of

$$\left\{ \begin{array}{l} \text{oars.} \\ \text{sails to catch the wind.} \\ \text{steam.} \end{array} \right.$$

CHAPTER SIX. MORE HOME-SEEKERS COME TO AMERICA

A Dutch Village That Became a Great City

The voyage of the "Half Moon." Captain Henry Hudson sailed across the ocean in a little Dutch ship called the "Half Moon." At last the small boat sailed into a fine harbor on the coast of America. A broad, deep channel led to the north. Up this channel, between high, rocky banks, and along wooded shores, sailed the "Half Moon."

Henry Hudson thought he had found a safe way to take his ship all the way through North America to the Pacific Ocean beyond. But after a time the captain noticed that there was a current in the water, and that the water itself was no longer salty, like the sea water. Then he knew he was on a large river. He named it the Hudson River, after himself. When he returned to Europe he told the people of Holland he had found the most beautiful land he had ever seen.

Trading with the Indians. The Dutch merchants had large numbers of good ships. The merchants wanted to carry goods to different parts of the world and trade with the strange people they found. So they sent men over to the river Hudson had found with packs of goods they thought could be traded to the Indians. In the packs were red blankets, kettles, cubes of red paint, beads, knives, and hatchets.

The Indians visited the white men, saw the wonderful goods they had, and were eager to have them for their own. They went back to their wigwams and gathered up many skins of beavers, minks, otters, and foxes. These they took to the white men and exchanged for the things in the packs. The Dutch merchants soon had hundreds of rich, soft skins for which they had given only a few dollars' worth of their goods. They made a fine profit in the fur trade they had begun.

Peter Minuit's island. The Dutch built forts and carried on their trade all up and down the Hudson River. Near the mouth of the river lay a long, narrow island on which was one of the Dutch forts. Peter Minuit, the Dutch leader, thought it would be a good idea to buy this island from the Indians. He spread out before the eager eyes of the Indians some of his gayest blankets and shiniest knives and hatchets. It is said that the value of the goods Peter Minuit offered was twenty-four dollars. That was not a very high price for a whole island. But the red men thought it a great offer. So they traded the island for the things offered them, and everybody was satisfied.

The Dutch named their new island Manhattan Island. It is the island on which stands today the greatest of the cities in the New World, New York City. How much do you think the island of Manhattan is worth today?

What things were the Indians eager to obtain from the white men?

What did the Indians have that the white men wanted?

Look at a map of the state of New York. Find Manhattan Island. Find the Hudson River and Long Island.

How Champlain Started a French Settlement at Quebec

A young French sailor. There lived in the country of France many years ago a keen, strong boy by the name of Samuel de Champlain. The boy wanted to be a sailor when he grew up. As soon as he was old enough he went to work on a small ship that sailed from town to town along the coast of France.

In a few years Champlain was known to be a good sailor. He began to serve his king on a large ship belonging to France. Even the leaders in Spain honored the skill and courage of the French sailor. They let him join them on a voyage to their towns in America.

While in the New World Champlain kept his eyes and his ears open. He was eager to learn all he could about the new lands, and about the animals and birds and plants to be found in them. The Indians interested Champlain, and he watched them and studied them whenever he had the chance. By the time he returned to France he knew more about the new land, America, than any other Frenchman.

Champlain's adventures in Canada. The ruler of France at this time was King Henry IV. He liked the careful way in which his captain, Champlain, had acted while among the Spaniards. When he decided to start a French settlement in America he made Champlain the leader of the settlers.

The young French leader crossed the ocean many times in his search for a good place to begin the French town in the New World. At last he led a band of settlers far up a great river called the St. Lawrence River.

On the north bank of this river he found a stony point high above the waters of the stream. Champlain thought this would be a good place for his fort. With the help of his men he built a fort having high, thick walls. Near the fort were built a number of log houses. The

tiny village on the great, cold river was called Quebec—
the name of the famous city which today looks down on
the St. Lawrence River from that very spot.

The Indians meant "village" when they used the
word Canada. The French thought they meant the land
along the river. Today the word Canada means the
land which lies north of our United States.

Champlain was eager to see for himself the large
lakes and the long rivers in the forests about his new
town of Quebec. He made friends with the many Indians who came to visit the white men's town on the
rock above the river. From these red visitors Champlain
learned all he could about the wild country farther up

the St. Lawrence. When he could he went with his Indian friends in their canoes far into the western country. He saw many broad lakes and winding rivers which no white man had ever before seen or even heard of.

The Indians liked the kind, brave Frenchman. Each spring they came in their canoes to visit him at Quebec. In their canoes were great bundles of thick furs. The white men who had come to live at Quebec carried on a good trade with their red neighbors.

Samuel de Champlain spent the rest of his life in his new French settlement. When he died the French king could boast that he owned in America a strong colony. Champlain will always be remembered as "The Father of New France."

How do you think you would treat people like the Indians in order to be good friends with them?

Why not try to draw a picture of Champlain in a canoe going up a river on one of his long journeys?

The Wise Quaker, William Penn

People with queer ideas. In England lived numbers of people who wanted to have peace everywhere in the world. They did not believe in fighting. They believed it was wrong and wicked for nations to go to war with each other. These people banded themselves together in a new church, calling themselves "Friends." Other people called them "Quakers."

The Quakers had other ideas that were thought queer

and that got them into trouble. To them it seemed wrong to spend money for costly and beautiful churches with tall steeples. God would be better pleased, thought the Quakers, if Christians met in plain little rooms and carried on church services in a simple way. In the minds of the Quakers it was clear that one person was as good as another in the sight of God. Each Quaker felt that he was the equal of every other person. None of the Quakers would take off his hat before the nobles or before the king himself.

Of course, the leaders in the fine churches and many of the great lords of the country did not like the Quakers. The Quakers received such bad treatment that they were eager to leave England to find a home where they would be at peace.

A rich young Quaker and his plans. At this time there was a boy in the great English school of Oxford by the name of William Penn. He wore fine clothes and had plenty of money. But when he heard the teachings of the Quakers, he decided that he would be a Quaker, too. His family and his friends thought that William must be crazy even to think of joining the poor, badly-treated Quakers. But join them he did.

Now Penn's father had been a famous leader in the navy of England. He had been a rich man, and when the king had needed money Penn had lent him a large sum. The money had not been paid back.

Young William got to thinking about this old debt

to his father. At last he went to the king and offered to take land in America in payment of the debt. The king was delighted. He had more acres of land in America than he had gold pounds in his treasury. The king's clerks unrolled the maps of America, and on one of them they marked out a great piece of land. Across this part of the map one of them wrote, "Pennsylvania," which meant "Penn's Woods." Young William Penn suddenly found himself the owner and ruler of millions of acres of wild land across the sea in America.

Maybe you can guess what William Penn wanted to do with all that land. Yes, he wanted to start a great settlement in America. He wanted to make a safe home in America for the unhappy Quakers in England and in the rest of Europe. He hoped that poor workers and their families from every land would come to Pennsylvania to get a new start in life.

Penn and the Indians. Soon people began to cross the Atlantic Ocean to Penn's colony. After a few years Penn himself crossed the sea to visit the new settlements in Pennsylvania. The ship he sailed in was called the "Welcome." It was a good name for the vessel, for the settlers gave their leader a glad welcome when his ship sailed up the Delaware River.

Penn wanted the Indians to be friendly to the people of Pennsylvania. Word was sent to the chiefs of the Indian tribes inviting them to pay a visit to the white leader. When they came they found Penn waiting for them with presents of blankets, shoes, stockings, and kettles. The red chiefs liked the gifts, and they liked the simple, kindly Quaker. After this Penn showed the Indians a writing which, he said, was a promise by both the white people and the red people to live together in peace. The Indians were pleased with the promise, or treaty, and made their marks on it to show that they would forever remain at peace with William Penn's people.

Before they went back to their villages the chiefs gave William Penn a belt on which were the figures of two men holding hands.

The city of brotherly love. On the banks of the Delaware River Penn laid out a new town and named it Philadelphia, "the city of brotherly love." The blocks between the streets were square, like the squares in a checker board. Penn planned to have trees to shade the streets and to have room for wide lawns about the houses.

After this, well pleased with his new colony, William Penn returned to England. The great city of Philadelphia is today often called "The Quaker City."

What were some of the beliefs of the Quakers?
Which words describe William Penn?

good	selfish	modest
kind	friendly	wise
peaceful	religious	wealthy
	foolish	

Lord Baltimore Sends Settlers to Maryland

One day in the year 1634 ships flying the flag of England sailed up the Potomac River. On the ships were three hundred English people who had been sent by Lord Baltimore to Maryland to make a settlement. Soon their leader, Leonard Calvert, a younger brother of Lord Baltimore, saw a piece of high ground on the bank of a small stream. He thought it would be a good place for a fort and a town.

When he went nearer to the place he found an Indian village on the ground he wanted. He bought the village and the land from the red men. The Indians moved away and the white people built their town where the Indians had once lived. They named their town St. Mary's.

The settlers and the Indians got along well together. The red men taught the English women how to make bread from corn. Some of the white men enjoyed long hunts in the forest with their new Indian friends.

Most of the people in the new colony were Catholics. They had left England because they were often ill-treated there. But in their American home they welcomed as neighbors all settlers who came to Maryland, no matter what religious ideas they had. If they were good Christian people they were given a chance to make their homes in the new colony. In a few years many small farms, and a few great farms, or plantations, lay in all directions about the town of St. Mary's.

A. Maryland, as you have just learned, was settled by people who had trouble in England over their religion. Name three other colonies that were started by people who also had been badly treated because of their religion.

B. Study a map and then fill in these sentences.
    South of Maryland was the colony of ____.
    North of Maryland a later colony was begun by ____.

New Southern Farms and Farm Crops

Can you find North Carolina and South Carolina on a map? The word Carolina comes from the name of one of England's kings, Charles II. Charles is written "Carolus" in Latin, and from Carolus comes Carolina.

Raising tobacco. When settlers came to live in North Carolina or South Carolina they nearly always became farmers. One of the crops they raised on their farms was tobacco. Tobacco grew well in Virginia and Maryland, as well as in the two Carolinas.

[104]

Raising a good crop of tobacco is hard work. Tobacco seeds are so tiny that they have first to be planted in small seed beds of earth mixed with wood ashes. When the young tobacco plants are a few inches high they are taken to the fields and there set out in rows. In early times this work was all done by hand. Worms injure tobacco plants. Years ago the farmers sometimes let flocks of turkeys go through the tobacco fields to find and eat the worms.

When the tobacco plants are quite tall, the tops are cut off. The plant then spreads and sends out larger leaves. After the leaves begin to turn yellow, the plant is cut off near the ground and placed with others on a

rack to dry. Later the leaves are stripped from the stalks and sorted. In the times your book tells about, the tobacco leaves were packed in great barrels ready to be shipped to England. There was so much work on the early tobacco farms that the farmers needed a great deal of help.

Eliza Lucas and her indigo farm. Perhaps you never heard of an indigo farm, but a little girl, Eliza Lucas, had one. Eliza moved to the new colony of South Carolina with her father and her invalid mother. They called their farm, or plantation, "Wappoo." Soon Eliza's father was called away to be a soldier of England. From one of the islands where he went he gathered and sent to Eliza some indigo plants.

No one had before tried to raise indigo plants in the colonies. But Eliza set out the plants, and they grew and became tall and strong. When Eliza's father heard about this he sent a man who knew how to make the dye, indigo, from the plants. This man cut the plants and began steeping them in water, at the same time beating them with a stick. As the plants slowly decayed, a deep violet color spread through the water. After the colored water had been treated and allowed to settle, it became a true indigo in color and made a very good dye.

The cloth makers in England were glad to learn that indigo could be made in one of England's colonies. A law was passed in England which said that anyone who would raise indigo plants was to have a special reward. In a few years great numbers of farmers had fields of indigo plants, and the making of indigo became an important industry. The young girl, Eliza Lucas, helped to start the making of indigo in the colony of South Carolina.

Rice farms. Some of the southern rivers had great swamps near them. One of the settlers sent to an island near Africa for some rice. This he planted in one of the swamps. The rice plants grew and gave a good crop. Soon large fields of rice were to be seen growing in the low, wet lands of South Carolina.

The swamps were often hot as well as wet. White men became sick working in such places. It was found that the colored people stood this work better than the white settlers. It was not long before large numbers of Negro slaves from Africa were busy at the work of tending the fields of rice.

Which phrases tell about rice, which tell about tobacco, and which about indigo?

made into dye
grew in swamps
seed mixed with wood ashes
steeped in water
tops of plant cut off
a little girl first planted it

James Oglethorpe and His Plans to Help Poor People

In prison for debt. People used to have strange ideas about debts. If a man owed money and could not pay his debt when it was due, he was thought to be a wicked person. Perhaps he had had a good reason for borrowing the money. Sickness, or being out of work, may have been the reason why he could not pay the debt. That made no difference: he was a wicked person just the same.

In many countries the laws said that persons who failed to pay their debts were to be put in prison. In England these prisons were crowded much of the time. Putting a man in prison for his debts seems to us today a very foolish way to treat him. For how could he ever get out of debt lying in some prison? The man to whom he owed the money could come to the prison and scold him, but that would not help get the debt paid.

Settlers in Georgia. James Oglethorpe was a kind-hearted Englishman. He felt sorry for the poor men of England who were in prison for debt. He asked the king to give him land in America where he could make a colony. After listening to Oglethorpe's plans the king granted to him a piece of land which later became the state of Georgia.

The king also allowed the kind Englishman to free persons who were in prison for their debts if they would

agree to go to America and live in the new colony. Oglethorpe said he would also send to Georgia any poor people who wanted to start life over in a new land. Each settler was to have a small farm, a house, a garden plot, seeds for planting, tools, a cow, and a pig. Soon the first shipload of poor people arrived in Georgia.

The leading town in the new colony was Savannah. Oglethorpe had the city laid out in squares, with room for large lawns and gardens. When the settlers had made enough money, they usually built comfortable homes for themselves and their families in this growing little city.

About one hundred years ago the leaders in different countries began to see how foolish it was to put people in prison for their debts. Most of the cruel old laws about debts were soon done away with.

A. In early times what treatment was sometimes given to persons who could not pay their debts? How did James Oglethorpe help these people?

B. Here is a matching game. Match each person's name with the sentence which tells about him. Number 1 matches c. Match the others.

1. Squanto
2. William Penn
3. Miles Standish
4. Peter Minuit
5. Pocahontas
6. Eliza Lucas
7. Ponce de Leon
8. Samuel de Champlain
9. Father Serra
10. Roger Williams

a. He believed in religious freedom.
b. He traded cheap jewelry and toys for an island.
c. He was an Indian who helped the Pilgrims.
d. He came to America in a ship called the "Welcome."
e. He helped build churches in California.
f. He searched for a fountain of youth.
g. She was an Indian friend of the settlers in Virginia.
h. This little settler got some of the farmers to raise a new crop.
i. This soldier protected some settlers.
j. He began a town on a great northern river.

C. Besides colonists from England, the settlers from what other countries are mentioned in these three chapters?

III. EVERYDAY LIFE IN LONG-AGO AMERICA

CHAPTER SEVEN. THE BOYS AND GIRLS OF EARLY TIMES

School Days

Do you suppose there were boys and girls among the groups of people who came to early America to make their homes? Of course there were. There were boys and girls on the "Mayflower." Children were on the ships that entered Boston Harbor, and on those that brought settlers to Pennsylvania, and to Maryland, and to the other southern colonies. What do you suppose they thought when they saw the strange, new shores before them? We wonder whether they were frightened when they saw their first Indians.

The parents of the colonial children were much like your parents. As soon as they had their houses built and were settled in their new homes, they began to think about schools and education for their children.

It was not long before many of the children, particularly those who lived in Puritan or Pilgrim homes, found themselves studying lessons in schools.

Going to school. Perhaps we should say that the boys found themselves going to school. No one cared much in those days whether girls went to school or not. People thought that a few lessons in reading and writing would not harm the girls. But they were sure that knowing how to cook and sew would do them much more good. In some places the girls went to school when the boys were not there. This meant go to school between six and half past seven in the morning, and between half past four and six in the afternoon.

One man said: "In winter it's too far to school for the girls. In the summer they should stay home and help in the kitchen."

But most fathers and mothers were eager for their boys to go to school. One mother once said to her son: "If God makes thee a good Christian and a good scholar, 'tis all thy mother ever asked for thee."

Let us look in on one of the schools where some of the colonial boys, at least, gained their education. In one end of the schoolroom there is a big fireplace. The logs for the fireplace were brought to the schoolhouse by the father of one of the boys. If he had not brought the wood when his turn came, his boy could not go to school any more—or would be placed by the schoolmaster on the bench farthest from the fire.

How the children studied their lessons. In this school that we are visiting, the benches where the boys sit face the wall. Along the wall is a wide board, and this board serves as a desk for the pupils. We do not see any maps or blackboards on the walls of the schoolroom. The children have a few scraps of coarse paper to write on. We find them doing most of their writing with ink, using a goose feather pen.

Perhaps the queerest thing about this school is that there are so few books. There are almost no books at all. The "book" the smallest boys are using is not a real book, even though it is called the "hornbook." It is a strip of board about the size of your hand. Over the thin piece of wood is placed a piece of paper on which have been printed the alphabet, some syllables, and, down below, the Lord's Prayer. Over the writing is fastened a thin piece of horn. The pupil can see the

letters and words through the horn, and the horn covering protects the paper. All the small children have horn-
books. Sometimes the handle of the hornbook has a
hole through it. A string run through the hole and
around the boy's neck keeps a careless lad from losing
his book.

Older boys are studying a book called the *New England Primer*. It is a real book and has about eighty pages
in it. If we examine one we shall see many pages containing letters of the alphabet and lists of words and
syllables. In the little book are also to be found a few
short prayers for the boys to learn and a number of

jingles which give good advice or, perhaps, tell a Bible story. One of the odd little poems goes like this:

> Zaccheus, he
> Did climb a tree
> His Lord to see.

When a boy could read simple sentences, write, and "do sums in arithmetic," he had about all the education he could get in the little log schoolhouses of early times.

Compare the schools of long ago with the one you attend. Why not make a chart? Begin this way:

	The schools of long ago	My school
the schoolhouse	made of logs	made of brick
how heated	?	?
the books	?	?

(Make a long list.)

Little Ladies and Gentlemen of the South

The boys and girls who grew up in the fine homes on the great southern farms, or plantations, must have had an interesting time. If we could have visited one of these homes—in Virginia, let us say—we should have found the big house surrounded with wide lawns and well-kept trees and bushes. Near by flows a wide, deep river.

If there is a boy in the family we are likely to see him dashing along on a little pony, for all the young gentlemen of the South wanted to be good riders. In his little, long coat, his brightly-colored breeches, his silk hose, and his buckled shoes, he looks very much like a small copy of his father. Riding just behind him we see a small colored boy, whose duty it is to go with his young master wherever the white boy goes.

Later in the day we may see this small southern gentleman studying his lessons. But he will not be in a

school with other children. He will be all by himself, or with only his brothers, in a quiet corner of the plantation home. His teacher lives in the house, too. He has been hired to stay there to teach the young master how to read and write and keep accounts.

If there are girls in the fine home they, too, will have lessons to study. They will learn the things that will help to make them ladies when they grow up. Some of their school hours will be given to music and dancing.

In the evenings, or when there is company, they will put on dainty little dresses that reach to their toes.

If our visit happens to be on Sunday, we shall see the planter and his family starting away to church. They have a long way to go. Mother and the smaller children will be seated in a carriage drawn by four horses. A Negro, dressed in a gay uniform, will sit in the driver's seat holding the reins and a long whip. Father and the older boys of the family will be riding on horseback beside the carriage.

Perhaps the most fun the little masters and mistresses have comes when they are free to play with the little colored boys and girls. Back of the big house stand rows of small cabins. In these cabins live the families of Negro slaves. The older colored people work on the great farm, or help about the plantation home. The small black boys and girls play about the small houses. They are pleased to have the white children come to play with them. There are so many servants to do the work that the small ladies and gentlemen in the plantation homes must find their lives easy and pleasant. Of course there were poor children in the southern colonies who did not lead the fine lives of the children we have just told about.

Try to find pictures of the southern boys and girls of long ago. Notice how they dressed. Perhaps you can find pictures of the homes of some of these children.

Will you make believe that you are a Puritan boy or girl of Boston, or Salem, or some other Puritan of the long ago? It is Saturday afternoon. Mother is hurrying about, baking and cooking meat. She needs your help, too. She wants you to help her get the house all spick and span, if you are a girl. And, if you are a boy, she expects you to keep the fireplace well filled with logs, with another great pile of logs laid by for more roaring fires. But why all this hurry on Saturday afternoon?

Puritan fathers and mothers wanted Sunday to be a day when only church matters took up their time. They thought it wrong to play or to do any work on Sunday. So the housekeepers hurried all day Saturday to prepare the food the family would need until Monday morning.

Not so very long after you waken on Sunday morning you will be reminded of what day it is. You will hear the ringing of a bell or, perhaps, a loud blast from a horn. Or, if there is neither a bell nor a horn in the church in your town, you may hear the thundering roll of a drum. No matter which, it tells you you must get up and get ready for church.

Soon you and your father and mother, and all your brothers and sisters, are hurrying along the village street in the direction of the church. When you get to the church door your father goes to sit on a bench at

one side of the church room. All the men are there.
Mother and the girls take seats with the other women
and girls on the other side. And you, if you are a boy,
will be put with all the other boys in a gallery.

This is a winter morning. Very soon you begin to
notice something. It is almost colder in the church than
it was outside. You can't see a sign of a stove or fireplace. Now you understand why your mother, before
she left home, filled a little iron box with live coals
from the fireplace and brought it along. She knows
very well how cold her feet would get without her foot
warmer.

Now the church service begins. There is no choir and

no organ, but all the people sing very slowly the verses of the old songs they know. You can see that your father and mother and all the other people have great respect for the preacher who now leads them in prayer. The prayer is long—longer than any you ever heard before. It may last an hour. When the prayer is finished the preacher begins his sermon. You are tired and very cold by this time. But if you are a good little Puritan you will sit very quiet and try not to show how you feel. Besides, there is a man with a long stick who may get after you if you fall asleep or move about too much.

The sermon may last two hours. After that is over you all go quietly outside and tramp away to your homes. As likely as not you will be told, after dinner, that there is to be another sermon in the afternoon.

Now that you have played at being a Puritan boy or girl, do you think the title of this story is a good one?

How Colonial Children Played

Boys and girls of colonial times had more work to do around home than you have. And when older persons were there, the children were supposed to be as quiet as so many mice. But of course children are just bound to play, no matter where they are or how they live.

Perhaps it will surprise you to learn that colonial boys and girls knew more little games than you do. And they played them oftener. Most of the games were the ones their grandfathers and grandmothers had played when they were children in England or Holland or some other old homeland across the sea. Some of the games must have been a thousand years old before they reached America.

Little girls, of course, had dolls. Some of these were wooden dolls, and had been cut out of a piece of soft pine wood. Some of the little girls used birch bark to make clothes for their dolls. Many dolls came to America from countries in Europe. Hundreds and hundreds of dolls made in Holland crossed the ocean in ships and at last found themselves in the arms of little colonial girls.

The children of early America liked to roll hoops and to spin tops. Most of the hoops and tops were home-made. The boys in those times, like many boys today, longed to own a good, sharp knife. Boys who had knives often could cut out good toys. They made willow whistles, pop-guns, windmills, and bows and arrows. Some of the boys used their fathers' tools to make hobby horses.

The girls, especially, knew many singing games. Here are four they liked:

> Ring around a rosy
> Here come three lords out of Spain
> The needle's eye
> London Bridge is falling down

How many of these do you know? Did you ever play them, and sing the words?

Other games that small boys and girls played together were hopscotch, stone tag, and wood tag. Cat's cradle was a quiet little game for two, and was best suited to be played indoors on a winter evening.

Just as boys often do today, the boys of long ago flew kites on the first windy spring day. Their marble games were almost like yours. They played ball with a soft, home-made ball and enjoyed such games as leapfrog as much as you boys do.

The Dutch boys and girls who came to America

brought with them their skates. The skates had wooden tops and iron blades. The winter sport of skating soon spread from the Dutch settlements to the towns and villages of their English neighbors. One colonist tells us that when he was a boy he wanted to own a pair of skates but had no money with which to buy them. So he made his skates. For blades he used two beef bones.

Do you think that colonial boys and girls had good times, even though their games were simple and their toys often home-made?

List the games mentioned in this story that you play today.

Would it be fun to learn about the dolls of the small girls of other countries? The teacher in the library will help you to find books that will tell about the dolls of other lands.

Did any of you boys ever cut a toy out of wood? Tell about it.

Ask your fathers and mothers—or, still better, your grandfathers and grandmothers—about the games they played when they were children. How many of them do you play?

Shall we use this cold winter evening to make a visit to the home of a long-ago American family? Here we are, then, after a long walk between the high banks of snow. We are at the kitchen door of a low, log house.

The fireplace. Our knock at the heavy plank door is answered, and we find ourselves in a big room. It is the kitchen, and it is much the largest room in the house. This should not surprise us, for in old times kitchens were not only kitchens but dining rooms and living rooms also. On this winter night all the members of the family we have come to visit are gathered in the kitchen. It is the only place where they can be cozy and warm.

We are quite sure to notice, first of all, the huge fireplace with its mass of blazing logs. The fireplace reaches almost across one end of the kitchen. We are given seats on a bench close to the fire. By bending over just a little we can watch the sparks as they go soaring up the wide chimney.

Hanging on chains in the fireplace are several large brass kettles. In these most of the food for the family is cooked. Perched on their long iron legs at one side of the fire are smaller iron pots, and a number of trivets, or three-legged iron stools. The stools can be pushed up close to the flames, and, just before meal time, they hold some of the metal dishes in which the food is to be

heated or cooked. Leaning in a corner of the fireplace
are some forks with very long handles. These are toast-
ing forks. Why are the handles so very long?

The kitchen. As we visit with the members of the
family we notice that each one is busy at some useful task. The father is making a pair of heavy shoes.
The mother is busy at her spinning wheel, while the
little girls are knitting mittens and stockings. One of

the boys is making an "Indian broom" by splitting
with his knife one end of a straight piece of yellow
birch wood. The evenings are long, and the settlers
cannot be idle when there is so much work to do.

While we are asking and answering questions, we
have time to look about the kitchen. The light is dim,
so we cannot see many things very clearly. Some of

the light comes from the flames in the fireplace. A part is given by candles set on small shelves. We learn that three kinds of candles are used in this home. Most of them are made of the fat of cows or sheep, called tallow. But there are on hand, also, a number of wax candles. Bees furnish the wax for some of these candles. A small, waxy berry that grows on the bayberry bush is also used for making wax candles. There is one small lamp in the kitchen. Its oil is whale oil. The little lamp is called a "betty lamp."

Besides the bench, or "settle," where we are seated, there is a great, heavy chair for father, a smaller one for mother, and crickets, or stools, for the smaller children. In one corner of the room stands a four-poster bed, with heavy curtains all around it. Shining dully on corner shelves and in cupboards can be seen a few pieces of silverware, and here and there some tinware. But most of the dishes we see are made of pewter.

After a good visit we put on our heavy jackets and wrap long, knitted scarfs about our heads and shoulders. Then, pulling on our heavy mittens, we say good night and tramp away toward home over the "crunchy" snow.

Behind us the family we have visited soon prepares for the long, cold night. First, the father carefully covers the fire with ashes so that it will not go out. Then mother gets the warming pan ready. This is a long-handled iron pan, about four inches deep, with an iron lid. After mother has filled the pan with coals from the fire, she hurries to the small beds where the children sleep. She passes the pan up and down, up and down, quickly, between the blankets to take away a little of the chill. Next, a great oak bar is set in place against the door, and one by one the candles are "snuffed," or put out. At last this settler's family of the long ago is ready for sleep.

A. Find the part of the story which helps you to understand these words and phrases?

snuffing the candle	betty lamp
warming pan	settle
bayberry bush	cricket
toasting forks	Indian broom

B. What did the early settlers use for—

light	brooms
heat	chairs
dishes	locks

TALKING WITH THE FISHERMEN

Many of the colonial boys and girls lived in villages right on the shore of the ocean. Almost every safe, deep harbor had a village on it. At times the waters of the harbors were almost covered with boats and small ships. These were the fishing vessels, and they belonged to the fathers and older brothers of the village children. Nearly every family in such a village made its living from the fishing.

"School, o-oh!" This sounds like a call to hurry to school, but it is not. It was the shout of a mackerel fisherman when he saw a "school" of mackerel. When this call sounded, the great nets were let down from the boats, spread out, and then lifted. If the fishermen were lucky, their nets would contain hundreds and hundreds of mackerel.

Cod, herring, and other fish were also captured with nets and hooks by the colonial fishermen. After the fish had been cleaned, they were dried and salted in sheds along the shore. After a time the fish were taken to markets in Europe or in the West Indies.

How happy the children were when the fishing boats came back to the harbor after their long voyages on the stormy ocean! We may be pretty sure they beat every one else in the village in the race to the wharves to greet the coming boats. There they met fathers and brothers home from the sea, looked at the cargoes of fish, and watched the fishermen as they wound their nets on great reels to dry.

Catching whales. Back to some of the little fishing towns came the whalers. The men who went away on voyages to capture whales were called whalers, of course. The stout ships they went in were called whalers, too. Every boy in the village felt proud if he could say that his father or a brother was a whaler.

In very early times the great whales came close to the shore where the settlers lived. Sometimes, even, they were washed up on the shore by the waves and could not get away. But in later colonial days hunting whales was likely to take the whalers on voyages of many thousands of miles.

When they came home with their ships filled with barrels of whale oil, they had wonderful stories to tell about going close up to the whales in small boats and driving their spears deep into the sides of the monsters. Often a wounded whale would tow a boat miles and miles through the sea before it gave up. Almost every boy hoped that he would sometime be brave and cool enough to become a whaler.

What different ways did the fishermen use in catching fish?

How were the fish prepared for the market, and where were they sold?

Try to find interesting facts about whales. Tell the class what you learn.

Work That Was Play

Most of the early settlers in the new America were poor people who had to work hard for a living. There were many tasks for the children as well as for their fathers and mothers. On the farms there were the chickens, pigs, and calves to feed and the cows to milk. The boys with their hoes could keep the weeds out of the patches of corn and potatoes. When the wheat and oats were cut in the fields, one of the tasks of the larger boys was to bind the grain into bundles.

In the village homes there was always wood to carry in to the fireplaces, and water to bring from the wells. Even small girls, in most colonial homes, helped clean and card wool, stirred the big kettle when soap was being made, helped dip candles, and aided their mothers in the many ways girls help their mothers today.

It doesn't seem likely that the boys and girls of long

ago liked their steady round of tasks any better than you do. But then, they did other helpful things that must have been fun for them.

In the summer time wild berries were to be gathered. Among the stumps in the fields wild strawberries could be found. In the brushy places the children found raspberries, and sometimes, in the swamps, they gathered the red cranberries. How pleased the mothers must have been to have the children come home from their berry picking with their wooden pails filled with wild berries!

Cool October evenings brought the corn huskings. The young people gathered on the floor of a barn and there husked the yellow ears of corn. This was useful work, too, and the boys and girls of long ago made a game of it.

On many of the small northern farms stood fine groves of maple trees. The farmers did not cut down

these trees, for the maple sap could be gathered in the early spring and boiled until it became maple syrup or maple sugar. The children were always on hand when the owner of the grove "sugared off," or finished the boiling of the sap. From the bottom of the kettle came warm, syrupy maple sugar for all. Then there was a gay time as the children played about among the big trees and circled about the roaring fire.

What is meant by the title of this short story?

Do you know the maple tree when you see it? Perhaps there are several kinds of maples in your yard or along the streets. Why not learn their names?

Did you ever gather wild berries? If you have, your experience will make a good subject for a written story.

Do you think the children of long ago had more interesting times than the children of today?

Make a list of all the new words and expressions in this chapter. There are a number of them. Test your classmates on your list. Perhaps they will want to test you on theirs.

CHAPTER EIGHT. COLONIAL FATHERS AND MOTHERS

A Rich Merchant of Boston

Some of the settlers in early America, as you already know, lived near the good harbors along the seashore. A number of these men owned large ships. The tall masts of the ships held great white sails. The captains and sailors of these ships sailed their vessels far out across the ocean.

Sometimes the ships made voyages up and down the coast of America, carrying wood, grain, or lumber from one town to another. At other times they sailed straight across the ocean to England with cargoes of fur, fish, or tobacco. When these ships came back from the mother country they brought cloth, guns, tools, furniture, and silverware to be sold to the people of America.

When William Phips was a boy he learned the trade of shipbuilding. After he had moved to Boston, and had married a rich woman who lived there, he became the owner of a number of fine ships. He sent his ships out on the ocean to carry on his trade for him.

One thing the merchants and their captains had to worry about was the pirates. The pirates owned fast-sailing ships. When the captains of the pirate ships dared, they followed and captured the ships of the merchants. Then they stole the goods of the merchants, and sometimes carried away or killed the people on board the captured vessels. William Phips often put cannons on his ships and, with the help of these big guns, sometimes drove the pirates away.

William Phips was rich, and his trading ships were making him still richer. But he was not satisfied. He wanted to make still more money, and make it faster than he had ever done before. So he thought of a plan. He knew that near one of the southern islands a Spanish ship loaded with riches had sunk where the water was not very deep. "If I could only raise that ship to the surface of the sea and get all that treasure!" thought William Phips. He took one of his ships and sailed down to the spot where the Spanish treasure ship had sunk. He tried to fasten chains to the old vessel and drag it up from the bottom of the sea. But it would not come up. Phips tried a second time, but still the treasure ship remained half-buried in the mud and sand of the ocean floor.

The king of England heard what William Phips was trying to do. He aided the Boston merchant with ships and men, and the third trial at lifting the old ship succeeded. On board William Phips found thirty-two tons of silver. After he had paid all who had lent him help he still had plenty of money left. The king was pleased and gave the merchant a title. After that he was always called "Sir William Phips."

He hardly knew what to do with all his money. He liked fine clothes, so he spent as much as he could for clothing. He dressed himself in satin coats with gold buttons, gay waistcoats, or vests, and olive-colored breeches. His powdered wigs were the best that his riches could buy, his stockings were of the finest silk, and the buckles on his shoes were of silver.

Here is a list of articles. Copy the things which you think were carried from the American colonies in the ships of the merchants.

tea	furs	pewter and silver dishes
rice	wheat	fish
lumber	coffee	indigo
silk cloth	tobacco	spices

BUILDING A LOG HOUSE

Did you ever see a house built all of logs? Here and there in our country families live in log houses even now. In early times log houses were common.

One man working alone could not build a good log house. His neighbors had to help him. First the men cut down trees, trimmed off the branches, and cut the tree trunks into the lengths they wanted. The colonial men with their sharp axes usually made the logs flat and smooth on four sides. Then they lifted the squared timbers and placed them one upon the other to make

the walls of the new house. In later times the settlers
cut the round logs in such a way as to make them
fit close together when placed on top of each other.

Long poles were cut and fitted to support a roof.

Sometimes the men put brush or grass over these poles to make a roof. This was called a thatch roof. Thin slabs of wood, called shakes, were often used to make a roof. At first some of the small cabins had only the ground for a floor.

It was hard to get glass for the windows of pioneer homes. Often the windows were only square holes cut through the log walls. These had heavy wooden shutters which were closed and fastened at night and during cold winter days. Of course, the shutters made the rooms dark and gloomy. Sometimes the people put a coating of grease on large sheets of paper and fastened the papers in the window openings. The light came in through the greased paper and made the log-cabin homes more cheery.

Try to draw a picture of a log house. Put a large fireplace at one end of your house.

Find a word in the story which means—

thin slabs of wood
a roof of brush or grass
pioneer home
wooden covering over a window

Traveling About in Early America

The people of our early America did not travel about a great deal. Of course, the sailors and the fishermen went on long voyages. And from village to village in the settlements went the peddlers. But the farmers and

their families seldom went on long trips. The roads and trails were so rough that not much pleasure was to be had in making journeys.

A governor's journey. One time the governor at Boston started on a trip. He wanted to go to Plymouth. He and his friends went on foot along a narrow trail through the woods. Indians showed them the way.

Soon they came to a stream. There was no bridge across it, not even a log. One of the Indians was a very strong red man. He took the governor on his back and carried him across the small river. All the rest of the journey, whenever the travelers came to a stream, the governor had a ride on an Indian's back.

When Plymouth was at last reached the governor and his friends were sore, tired, and hungry. It was only forty-five miles from Boston to Plymouth, but the travelers had spent two long hard days on the trail.

Now if governors, even, had such a hard time when they traveled, can we wonder that common people stayed close to their homes?

"Ride and tie." As time went by more and more of

the settlers owned horses. Sometimes two men, having only one horse between them, went on a journey. Here is the way they managed: one man started on foot, while the other rode the horse. Of course, the man on horseback made the better time. After he had ridden on ahead for a long distance he got down, tied his horse, and tramped on along the road. When his traveling companion reached the horse he untied him, got into the saddle, and rode on after the other man. He passed him by on the trail, galloped on a good distance, then got off, tied the horse, and, as the first man had done, went ahead on foot.

The two men kept this up, ride-and-tie, ride-and-tie, until their journey was finished. By this means a long distance could be covered in a day.

A horseback journey. Of course, on short trips, a strong horse often carried two, or even three, people on his back. If you had been a child in those early times, perhaps you would more than once have been the third "passenger" on a horse's back. In the saddle, and holding the reins, let us suppose, is your father. Behind father on the horse is mother. She sits on a pillow, or "pillion," as it was called, and hangs on by wrapping her arms about father's waist. You are perched in front of father, almost on old Dobbin's neck. You are between father's arms, but if you are still afraid of falling off you can grip your fingers in the horse's mane. You surely do not have a very comfortable seat, but you will not object. After all, even this bumpy ride is better than staying at home alone.

Can you write out these sentences, filling in the blanks?

1. The part of a harness which fits over a horse's head is called the ____.

2. The leather strips used in guiding a horse are called the ____.

3. The steel piece that goes in the horse's mouth is called a ____.

4. The high front part of a saddle is called its ____.

5. The rider rests his feet in the ____.

Launching the Ship

Governor John Winthrop of Boston decided that his colony needed a ship. He hired men and set them at work building the first sailing vessel ever built in Massachusetts.

The men first went up a river until they found tall, straight pine trees. These they cut and brought down to the shore of the bay, where the logs were made into masts for the new ship. Then oak trees were cut down, and their trunks were fitted to make the frame of the vessel. With tools called augers the men bored holes through the oak timbers and then fastened them firmly together by driving wooden pins into the holes.

After the hull of the ship had been finished, pitch from the pines was brought, heated, and poured into all the seams and joints to prevent the ship from leaking. Soon the new vessel was ready to be launched.

When the people of Boston gathered to watch the launching of the ship, they found it resting in a hollowed, slanting trough made of timbers. One of the men was busy covering the floor of this trough with grease. Then two men took a long saw and cut through a stout log that held the ship in its trough, or "ways," as shipbuilders call it. All at once there was a shout, and the vessel slid down its ways and into the bay with a great splash.

While the new ship floated at anchor in Boston Harbor, the workers built tiny cabins on its deck and fitted it with sails. Soon it was ready to sail away on voyages along the coast.

John Winthrop's little ship was named the "Blessing of the Bay." The people were proud of the new vessel, and soon saw how useful ships could be to them. The fishermen and the merchants all needed ships. Whalers wanted strong vessels for their long voyages. Before many years had passed, a thousand ships, so it is said, were owned by the people in England's colonies.

Sailors use many words and terms that have only to do with ships and with voyaging at sea. A few are found in this story. Make a list of them. Here are others:

starboard	larboard
mainmast	bowsprit
fore	aft
lee	windward

Why not find their meanings and, perhaps, add to the list?

A DUTCH RENT DAY

Dutch farmers in America. In Chapter Six there was a story about the Dutch traders, and how one of them bought the whole of Manhattan Island from the Indians for twenty-four dollars' worth of goods. This is another story about the Dutch people in America.

Not long after the Dutch merchants began their trade along the Hudson River, numbers of Dutch farmers began their settlements along the wide, deep river. Most of these farmers were very poor. They had not been able to pay for the passage of themselves and their families on the ships coming to America. Besides, they had not been eager to cross the sea and make their

homes in the new land. But when the men learned that they could rent land for a small amount of money, and that each of them was to receive from his landlord a small house to live in, some cows, and the tools he would need as a farmer, they made up their minds to come to America. The landlords gave the settlers free passage on the ships.

Paying rent with pigs and chickens. The Dutch farmers found good land in the little valleys. They liked the beautiful river flowing past their homes between its steep banks. Once a year came rent day. On that day the settlers and their families traveled to the big house where the landlord lived. Some of them carried crates of geese or chickens. Others drove pigs or calves before them along the narrow roads. The women carried jars of butter and baskets of eggs. All these

things went to the landlord as rent for his lands. After the rent had been paid, the people gathered on the lawn and had a dance and a feast.

The rent for the good land was small, but the people did not like to pay it. They wanted to own land of their own. Besides, there were many things they could not do without first asking the landlord. They could not hunt, or fish, or cut down a tree, or go away from the land unless he allowed them to. In a free land like America the Dutch farmers wanted to be truly free. When they were able to do so they moved away to farms of their own.

Pretend that you are one of the Dutch farmers in America. Write a letter to a friend in Holland telling about things that you like, and those that you do not like in your new home.

LET'S GO SHOPPING

How can you shop unless there are stores? In early America there were few stores and shops.

The peddlers. The people of those times did not need stores as much as we do. They made in their homes, or raised on their farms, nearly everything they needed. They made their shoes and clothes and hats. Much of the furniture was home-made. The women dried apples and berries for winter use, and made soap and candles and quilts and curtains. The farms furnished wheat and corn, eggs and chickens, milk and butter.

All this makes it clear that the settlers in the early colonies did not need to visit the stores as often as we do now.

Sometimes the stores came to them. That is, peddlers traveled from home to home carrying great packs of goods on their backs. The things the peddlers took from their packs were sure to interest the mothers and the children. If there was any money in the house, the peddler was quite sure to make a sale. Some peddlers took butter or eggs or maple sugar for their goods.

The plantation "shoppers." Many of the southern owners of the great rice or tobacco farms had a curious way of doing their shopping. They shopped in England. No, they did not cross the ocean to buy the things they wanted. This is the way it was done: Each year a ship came from England and sailed up the broad river that led almost to the rich farmer's door. The ship came for the tobacco or rice he had raised on his plantation. Before the ship went away with its cargo, the planter and his wife made out a list. On the list were named the many things they wanted from the shops and stores of England. Perhaps they put down such items as silverware, silk stockings, wigs, rugs, jewelry, and yards of satin and other cloth. Most of the planters liked to ride and hunt; so they often ordered from England riding horses and saddles. Some of them even ordered packs of English hunting dogs.

When the list was finished it was handed to the captain of the ship. When the captain reached·England with his ship, he gave the list to a man there. It was this man's duty to see about selling the tobacco or rice. After he had done this he went out and shopped for the planter in the far-away colony, sending the goods across the sea on the first ship that sailed.

George Washington and his wife, Martha, on their plantation home at Mount Vernon, did much of their shopping in the way we have told about.

What is a peddler? Did you ever see one? Ask your grandmothers about the peddlers they used to see.

Tell how the ladies and gentlemen of the southern plantations did their shopping.

The three main ideas in this story are:

Making things at home
Buying from peddlers
Shopping in England

Make an outline by writing some little ideas under the three main ideas.

A SERVANT'S STORY

When poor people in Europe heard about the good soil in America and the fine timber and the fish and game, they wanted to come here to live. But how could they ever get money to pay for their passage on board a ship crossing the ocean? In a story in Chapter Six there is one answer to that question. One of the stories in this chapter gives another answer. And there was still another way to get to America in those days, even though purses were empty. Here is the story one man told.

A free ride across the ocean. I wanted to come to America, but I earned so little money that I could not see how I ever could save any of it to pay my way across the ocean. Then one day I heard wonderful news. I heard that a ship captain would take good, willing workers across for nothing. I could hardly believe it, but it turned out to be true. Soon I found myself on a ship sailing away to the west. That ship was crowded with people like myself. Some of them were married people, and they had their children with them. We were all poor. The ship was beaten about on the sea by the wind and waves, and it was many weeks before we sighted land. We were a dirty, sick, tired lot of people when at last the ship sailed up the Delaware River and anchored not far from the city of Philadelphia. The trees along the banks of the river, the green fields, and what we could see of the neat little city looked like heaven to us.

But was it a free ride? We could not leave the ship. We waited, and soon men began coming on board to look us over. Some of the men looked like rich farmers. Others seemed to be shipbuilders and merchants. They talked to us, first to one and then to another.

Now and then one of the visitors would lead one of my fellow passengers to the captain's cabin. There, so I learned, he paid the captain the money it had cost to bring that passenger across the ocean. The man whose passage he had paid had to sign his name to a paper. The paper said that the passenger was to work for the man who had paid the money for as many as five or six years. For this work he was to receive nothing but his food and shelter. He was to be a servant. After he had finished his years as a servant he was free to do as he pleased.

I must have looked very sick and weak, for no one wanted me at first. I watched, and several times I saw a father "sell" himself to one man, while his wife, perhaps, became the servant of another man, and his children of still another. Children had to stay with their new masters until they were twenty-one years old. I wonder if these families ever got together again?

Some of the sickest among the passengers died while they waited for someone to pay their passage and take them away.

At last a man decided he could get enough work out of

me in five years to repay him the few pounds it cost to bring me to Philadelphia. Since that time I have been working on his large farm near the city. When my five years are up I hope I can get a small farm and be my own master. It has been a hard life—but, anyway, here I am in America.

Was the man who told this story truly free, in the way that you and your father and mother are free? Do you think this story proves that many people were eager to come to America to live?

A. Rule a sheet of paper as you see this one ruled just below. Then compare life in early America with life today. Start like this:

	Then	*Now*
the ships	small sailing ships	large steam vessels
traveling		
trading		

Make a long list.

B. Tell a story, just as though you were there, about—
   launching a ship
   building a log house
   coming to America to be a servant
   going to sea as a sailor
   making a horseback journey

CHAPTER NINE. EARLY-DAY STORIES

THE ADVENTURES OF A BOY PRINTER

In early times there lived in the small city of Boston a soap maker and tallow chandler. That is, besides making soap he made and sold tallow candles. He had to work hard, for he had a large family to take care of. The youngest child of the family was named Benjamin. Benjamin was a lively, fun-loving boy.

As the boy grew older he learned to help his father in the shop. But he did not like soap-making and candle-making. He did not care to stay in the dirty, bad-smelling little shop. He thought he would become a sailor and travel away to far countries in a fine ship.

The soap maker worried about his youngest son, Benjamin. Then he thought of a plan. To keep Ben from running away to sea he decided to make him a printer. There were not many printers in the America of that time. The first types and the first printing press had been brought across the ocean in the year 1639, but not many books and newspapers had been printed. One of Ben's older brothers, James, had a newspaper in Bos-

ton, so the young boy went to work in James's printing shop.

The young printer. Most people thought that printing was a very poor business. Boston had two newspapers, but the people there felt that one was enough. Some thought that one newspaper was enough for all the thirteen colonies. James had to work hard to make enough money to live on.

But young Ben liked the work in a printing shop. He tried his hand at writing some things for the paper. He did not sign his name to his stories, but pushed them under the door where they would be found. James's friends liked what the boy had written, and the stories were printed in the paper. Ben was quite proud of himself.

Ben and his brother James did not get along together very well. At last Ben made up his mind to run away. He sold the books he owned and with the money paid his passage to New York on a ship.

Getting started in Philadelphia. New York turned out to be a poor place for a young printer to find work. Ben could not find anyone who would give him a position. When he learned that a printer in Philadelphia needed a helper, he decided to go to that city.

Making up his mind to go to Philadelphia and really getting there, so Ben found, were two different matters. A storm almost wrecked the boat that carried him across the bay from New York to the shore of New

Jersey. From there it was a long, hard journey along a rough road which led to Philadelphia.

The young printer was wet, cold, and hungry when he reached the city. His extra clothes were stuffed in his pockets. In one of them, also, was a "Dutch dollar" and a "shilling copper." That was all the money Ben had.

The hungry boy stepped into the first bakery he saw. There he asked for threepenny's worth of bread. He was given three big, puffy rolls. Away he went down Market Street carrying one roll under each arm and eating the third one.

A girl standing in the doorway of a fine home smiled when she saw the untidy young fellow passing by. Years afterward she became the young printer's wife.

Benjamin, after he had eaten his loaf, went into a Quaker meeting house. Quaker meetings are very quiet, so Ben fell asleep. The kind Quakers did not bother him, and he had a good sleep. After that he went on down the street and, before very long, found work with a printer.

Perhaps by this time you have guessed what Benjamin's other name was. Yes, this story is about Benjamin Franklin, and how it happened that he became a printer in Philadelphia. It did not take him long to prove that he was a good printer and a good writer, as well. Very soon he had a printing shop of his own. And not many years passed before he was the best-known printer and the best-liked writer in all the American colonies.

After he had made enough money he spent most of his time helping his city, his state, and the new nation that was forming in America. Other stories in the book will tell more about Benjamin Franklin.

Prepare to tell the story of the young printer. Think what you will say on each of these three points·

Benjamin Franklin as a boy in Boston
The journey to Philadelphia
Getting started as a printer in the strange town

The Knights of the Golden Horseshoe

Governor Alexander Spotswood of Virginia colony wanted to know what the western parts of his colony were like. Virginia was so big, and reached so far to the west, that none of the white settlers knew what lay beyond the edge of the last western farms. Most of them were afraid to go far away from the ocean shore or the banks of the broad rivers. They knew that off to the west there were woods and wild animals and Indians, but they knew little more about that country. The governor of Virginia wanted to know more than that.

A famous journey. Governor Spotswood asked a large number of the Virginia gentlemen to go with him to explore the forests and mountains. The men first gathered at the governor's house and then set out toward the west. Each one of them was mounted on his

best horse. With the gentlemen were many servants who cooked the meals over big camp-fires along the way and set up the tents for their masters. Day by day the governor and his friends rode along the trails toward the wild country.

The horses got along very well in the soft soil of the level country. But after a while the travelers came to places where there were many rocks. The sharp stones hurt the horses' feet, so the men had to stop while the blacksmiths shod the animals. After that they went on once more.

Soon the governor and the men with him saw before them the high tops of mountains. From a distance the mountains looked blue. The men named the long range of mountains the Blue Ridge. You can find that name on the maps of western Virginia today.

The riders had a hard scramble up to the top of the Blue Ridge. Beyond they could see a deep, beautiful valley. Still farther on they could see another long line of mountains. It was a grand sight. The men dreamed of the time when settlers would make their homes in the great valley between the mountains.

The golden horseshoes. When the Virginians got back to their homes Governor Spotswood thought it would be a good idea to have a reminder of this first journey to the mountains. He sent to England and ordered made a number of small golden horseshoes. To each of the gentlemen who had gone with him on the journey he gave one of these horseshoes. The men were proud and happy to have these emblems. They treasured them carefully and passed them on to their children. From that time on the men who had made the famous journey were known as the Knights of the Golden Horseshoe.

Near the end of this story is the word "emblem." From the way it is used, can you tell what it means?

Why did the governor choose a horseshoe for an emblem?

Did you ever climb a high hill just for the fun of climbing it?

Did Governor Spotswood have any other reasons for climbing to the top of the Blue Ridge?

BURIED TREASURE

In late colonial times hundreds of fine ships voyaged
here and there on the Atlantic Ocean. Some of them had
on board tobacco, or furs, or sugar, or molasses. The
Spanish ships had the richest cargoes of all. They carried
from America to Spain the gold and silver from Mexico
and Peru.

All these valuable cargoes in the big merchant ships were too much for the honesty of some of the men of that time. These men turned pirate. A pirate is a man who robs ships on the ocean. The pirates had to have ships, too, of course, and with these they chased the merchant ships, captured them, and stole whatever they found in the ships. For many years the pirates had things very much their own way. It was dangerous for honest men to send their ships to any distant port.

Captain Kidd had always been thought a good, honest Englishman. He had fought for his country against France. So the king sent Captain Kidd out on the ocean in a fine ship to hunt pirates. But the captain soon gave up hunting pirates. He turned pirate himself, and began capturing the merchant ships of all nations.

You may be sure that the King of England was very angry with Captain Kidd. He was more eager to capture Kidd than a dozen of the other pirate captains.

The ships of England began hunting everywhere for Captain Kidd. After a while the "turncoat" was captured, taken to England in heavy chains, and hanged.

A year or two before all this happened, some people had seen Captain Kidd go on shore on Long Island, not far from the city of New York. They thought that perhaps he had buried some of his stolen gold on the island. After the captain was dead, searchers began digging here and there on Long Island for the buried treasure. And sure enough, they found it—or a part of it. They found almost a hundred thousand dollars. That is a great deal of money, but some people thought that Captain Kidd had buried much more than that.

From that day to this searchers have been hunting for the rest of Captain Kidd's buried treasure. But no one has been able to find any more of the pirate's gold.

Find in the story one word to finish each sentence.

1. Robbers on the sea are called ____.
2. The goods carried on a ship is called the ____.
3. The place where ships come to land is called a ____.

A March Through the Forest

There was a great stir in the log-cabin village of New-town, in the summer of 1635. Newtown was very close to Boston and it was well named, for the town was only four or five years old. But nearly all of the people were packing up and getting ready to go away.

"Yes, there's good land, and plenty of it, in the western river valley," the men of Newtown kept telling each other. "All who have been there agree on that. If we stay here on this poor soil we shall always be poor, like the soil. Our preacher, Thomas Hooker, says so. He is going with us."

The strong, active boys and girls of Newtown felt very grown-up and important. They were not going to make the long journey to the Connecticut River in boats with the small children and some of the mothers and the household goods. No, they were going to march with the men through the woods to the new home.

Following the Indian trail. At last the march was begun. Far ahead on a dim old Indian trail were the young men with the herd of one hundred sixty cattle. Next came the pack horses with men or boys leading them. Behind the horses tramped the strong young women and most of the boys and girls. Bringing up the rear, or stepping softly through the bushes on either side of the trail, were most of the men. They carried heavy packs and had their guns in their hands. They watched anxiously for any signs of an Indian attack.

At first the journey was fun for the boys and girls.
Often they darted into the bushes to gather flowers or
to chase squirrels. But after a time some of the younger
ones grew tired. Their fathers picked them up and
placed them on top of the packs carried by the horses,
or, perhaps, on the broad backs of some of the gentlest
of the oxen.

Each night the travelers stopped in the woods and

ate and slept beside big camp-fires. A few of the men stayed awake all night and walked round and round the herd of cattle to keep them from straying away. After two weeks of marching through the woods, the people of Newtown came out on the banks of the Connecticut River. They had walked a hundred miles.

New towns and new farms. All the settlers were happy when the boats came bringing the mothers and the smaller children. Soon a number of snug log cabins stood on the bank of the river. Next, around the houses was built a high fence of sharpened timbers. This fence made a fort to protect the people if the Indians should make an attack.

The rich land near the new village was divided among the men. Each man also had a share in the fine timber near by, and in the land that was good for pasture for the cattle. Then the men held a meeting, made rules, and began to govern themselves. They were all glad that their minister, Thomas Hooker, was with them in their new settlement.

The new village was named Hartford. It is today one of the fine cities of Connecticut. Many towns of New England were started in much the same way that Hartford was begun.

1. Thomas Hooker was the ____.
2. The new village that he settled was called ____.
3. Hartford is in the state of ____.
4. The mothers and small children made the journey in ____.
5. The men and boys reached the new settlement by ____.

John Eliot, the Teacher of the Indians

John Eliot was one of the Puritan ministers who came to America in early times. He liked the Indians and wanted to do what he could to help them.

Numbers of Indians lived in Massachusetts, Connecticut, and the other northern colonies. There would have been more except for the terrible disease which had swept through the Indian villages a few years before the white men came. You learned something about this sickness in Chapter Five.

Most of the Indians were like Samoset and Squanto, and wanted to be friends with the white people. But at times some of the Indian tribes became very angry at the white settlers and fought with them.

John Eliot wanted the red men and the white men to be at peace. He felt it to be his duty to talk to the Indians about the Christian religion. The first thing John Eliot did was to learn the language of the Narragansett Indians. Then he went to these Indians and called them together. He told them about the religion the white people followed, and urged the red men to give up their ways and become Christians.

Then John Eliot thought of something else to do. He worked very hard and at last was able to write the language of the Narragansetts—something which, of course, no Indian was able to do. After that he wrote parts of the Bible in the Indian language.

The Indians liked John Eliot. Many of them tried hard to do what he wanted them to do. They left their wigwams and their villages and started new Indian towns where they could all be together and together learn the lessons of the Bible. Some of the red men, in order to please their white friend, built themselves log houses instead of wigwams. Others set out apple trees and plum trees and learned from John Eliot how to raise better crops of corn and vegetables.

Many of the Indians never forgot what the kind white man had taught them. They learned to live almost as the white men did.

John Eliot was a missionary to the Indians. Do you understand what the word "missionary" means?

Are there any missionaries at work today? In what countries are they carrying on their work?

Were the settlers always as kind to the Indians as John Eliot tried to be?

The Last Dutch Governor

Governor Peter Stuyvesant. The ruler of the Dutch colony in America had a very bad temper. He also had a wooden leg. When he was angry—which was much of the time—he stamped about on his wooden leg, shouting and making a great racket, and frightening every one within sound of his voice. The governor was severe in punishing persons who did even small wrongs. He was cruel to the Quakers when they came to his colony. The old governor meant well in many things, and he was true to the Dutch who had sent him to rule the colony. But the people learned to hate him.

A surprise for Peter Stuyvesant. The Dutch towns and farms were near the mouth of the Hudson River and along the fine valley of the wide, deep stream. The lands claimed by the Dutch were called New Netherlands. The number of white people in the colony was not large, but the Dutch merchants made money from the fur trade with the Indians.

Now England also claimed the land where the Dutch had settled. They said that an English sailor, John Cabot, had seen the country long before Henry Hudson sailed his little ship, the "Half Moon," up the Hudson River and claimed the land for the Dutch.

Imagine the feeling in New Amsterdam, the chief Dutch town, when, one day, the people looked down toward the ocean and saw three English ships coming

into the bay. On the ships were many large cannons
and several hundred English soldiers. The ships and the
soldiers had been sent to capture the Dutch colony.

Peter Stuyvesant was more angry and noisy than
ever before. He cried that he would rather die than
surrender New Netherlands to the English. He tried
to get his people to fight. But not many of the people
felt the way the governor did. Some of them no doubt
thought that here was a good way to get rid of a mean
governor. They would not lift a hand to save the colony.
Peter Stuyvesant stormed and stamped about, but of

course he could do nothing alone. So he had to give up. After that there was no longer in America any New Netherlands. The town of New Amsterdam became New York.

Turn back to Chapter Six and read again the story about Henry Hudson. Then plan a talk about the Dutch colony, being sure to put in something about each of these topics:

How Henry Hudson found and named the Hudson River
The Dutch traders and the Indians
Buying Manhattan Island
The last Dutch governor

The Boy Surveyor

A Virginia schoolboy. A man by the name of Hobby was a teacher in a school in Virginia many years ago. The school was called an "old field school" because it stood in the corner of an old field where the soil had become so poor that it would no longer raise a crop of tobacco.

We are interested in Mr. Hobby's school because of a brown-haired, blue-eyed boy who was a pupil in it. He was larger and stronger than most of the boys of his age. His name was George Washington.

It is said that George Washington was a good boy in school. Mr. Hobby did not send home report cards as teachers do now. If he had, Mrs. Washington would have seen a big "A" on George's card. He would have had a good grade in arithmetic, too. But it seems likely that he would have almost failed in spelling.

At recess time George Washington was a leader among the boys. He could outrun and outjump most of them. He liked to play "soldier." He was always the captain, and the other boys were his soldiers.

Mount Vernon. Lawrence Washington was George's half-brother. He was many years older than George. Lawrence laid out a fine farm on the Potomac River and named it Mount Vernon after one of his old commanders in the English navy. On a high piece of ground near the river he built a good house.

Little did young George Washington think, when he used to visit at Mount Vernon, that soon the beautiful spot on the Potomac River would be his. But it was true, for soon Lawrence became sick and died, leaving Mount Vernon to his younger brother.

In the western forest. One of the rich men of Virginia owned a great piece of wild land among the mountains far back from the plantations. He did not know much about his land. He decided to have it surveyed, that is, have it marked off so that he would know just what he owned. There were several good surveyors in Virginia, but the rich man hired a boy to do his surveying for him. The boy was George Washington, then sixteen years old.

But you will remember that George Washington was good in arithmetic, and surveyors need to know how to

figure and not make mistakes. Then, too, he was strong, and he already knew a great deal about land and about the work of a surveyor. Soon George Washington and the men who were to help him were far away in the forest.

The young surveyor traveled day after day through the woods. He made straight lines across the land owned by the rich planter. He noticed what kinds of trees grew in the forest. In the notes that he put down in a book he told about the places where the soil was rich. On maps he showed where the mountains and rivers were.

Each night George Washington and his companions camped in the forest. Now and then they visited an Indian village, and sometimes the red men came to see the boy surveyor in his camp. The Indians liked Washington because he was so serious and honest and treated them so fairly. The man who hired George Washington as a surveyor was much pleased over the clear report that was at last handed to him.

George Washington learned a great deal while he was in the forest. He learned to be cool and careful, how to deal with the Indians, and how to get along with them. When he returned from his journey as a surveyor he was almost as much at home in the woods as the Indians themselves.

Finish these sentences.

1. George Washington's first school was called an "old field school" because ____.
2. George Washington was hired to be a surveyor because ____.
3. The Indians liked the young surveyor because ____.
4. Washington's life as a surveyor helped him later on because ____.
5. The men who went to the mountains with Governor Spotswood were afterward called ____.
6. Benjamin Franklin was born in ____, but spent most of his life in ____.
7. People have often hunted for ____'s buried treasure.
8. The Dutch colony was near the ____ River. Its last governor was ____.
9. People who mark out land are called ____.
10. The Dutch called the chief town in their colony ____. The English changed the name to ____.
11. The missionaries wanted the Indians to become ____.
12. The name of an early English missionary is ____.
13. Some Puritans left Massachusetts and moved to ____. Their preacher was ____.
14. When ____ died he left his home, ____, to George Washington.

IV. FINDING THE WESTERN LAKES AND RIVERS
CHAPTER TEN. STORIES ABOUT THE FRENCH LEADERS IN AMERICA

A FRENCH BOY OF MONTREAL

The most exciting news came one day to a young French boy named Pierre. He learned that he was to go in a ship all the way from his home in France to the new French settlements in America.

Soon Pierre's voyage began. His ship tossed for many weeks on the stormy ocean. Then the vessel sailed into the mouth of a wide river—so wide that at first Pierre could not see the shores on either side. The river, as Pierre and all Frenchmen knew, was the St. Lawrence River. Slowly, as the ship went forward, the river narrowed. At last the ship anchored before the new little town of Montreal, far up the cold river.

Getting acquainted with the Indians. The French boy was interested in everything he saw in his new home. But best of all he liked to watch the Indians as they

came and went in their canoes, or pitched their wigwams along the banks of the river. The Indians brought
their furs to the French traders. They were friendly,
smiling red men, and what a sight they made as they
walked without a sound in their robes of rich fur and
their beaded moccasins. Pierre never tired of watching
the tall, straight, copper-hued Indians who came to
visit Montreal.

A prisoner of the Indians. But there were other red
men who were not so friendly to the "palefaces," as
Pierre soon found out.

One day he and two other boys went hunting.

"Get back early. Remember, our enemies, the Iroquois, are always prowling about," the boys had been
warned.

But they forgot the warning. The sun went down and
they were still far from the fort at Montreal. Suddenly
a band of painted warriors rose from the bushes and
rushed upon the three boys. Pierre's two companions
were killed. Pierre was carried away a prisoner. For two
weeks he was dragged along by the Indians until they
came to one of their villages.

The Iroquois hated the French. Even the women and children felt like killing every Frenchman they saw. They had no mercy on Pierre, and he was battered and bruised until he almost wished he were dead, too.

Then a kindly old Indian couple adopted the white boy. They had lost a son about Pierre's age, and they wanted some one to take his place. From that time on Pierre began to have a pleasant time in the village of the Iroquois.

Pierre's escape. Two years passed, and Pierre, with his hair dressed as the young Indians wore theirs, and with his paint and feathers and moccasins, looked so much like a real Indian that only the sharpest of eyes

could have seen the difference. But Pierre was still a white boy. He liked his red friends and his adopted father and mother. But he wanted to be with his own people. He decided to run away.

In a hollow tree near the village Pierre hid a strong pair of moccasins and a supply of food. One morning he walked into the bushes, hurried to his tree, took what he had hidden there, and dashed away. He traveled alone through the woods for more than a hundred miles before he found white friends. At last he returned to his home in Montreal. Another story in this chapter will tell more about Pierre.

Perhaps you would like to turn back to Chapter Six and read about Champlain and how he began the French colony on the St. Lawrence River. This was the colony to which Pierre came from France.

What new things do you learn about Indians in this story?

What are meant by "beaded moccasins"?

If you remember the story about Champlain, you can answer this question: Why did the Iroquois Indians dislike the Frenchmen?

Tell the story of Pierre, "the white Indian boy," as he might have told it when he got back to Montreal.

FINDING THE ANSWER

The Indians who came to the French towns to trade kept telling the white men about the rivers and lakes and forests where they lived. The Frenchmen grew eager to see for themselves the places the Indians told about. Soon the boldest of the white men paddled away in the canoes of their Indian friends toward the far-distant places where the red men made their homes.

Soon the eager Frenchmen were on lakes and rivers no white people had ever seen before. One traveler discovered Lake Huron. Another went with the Indians to the shore of Lake Michigan. The canoes of other Frenchmen carried them to the largest of all the Great Lakes, Lake Superior.

One day a group of Frenchmen near the western end of Lake Ontario heard a great roaring sound, and soon they came out on a high place among the rocks from where they could see Niagara Falls. One of them, Father Hennepin, drew a picture of the falls. It was the first picture ever made of the great waterfall.

Learning about a great river. Every now and then the white men heard the Indians speak of a very large river which flowed away through the forest. The red men did not know where the river began, or where it emptied into the sea. They called the river a name which meant "father of waters."

Louis Joliet and Father Marquette set out in two canoes to find this river. They wanted to travel down the river, when they found it, and learn where it reached the ocean. The two men and their companions traveled along the edge of Lake Michigan for a long distance, and then pushed their canoes up a winding river. Then at last they lifted the canoes from the water, carried them across a wide marsh, and set them down in the clear current of another stream.

In a few days this new stream carried the two canoes to a place where the travelers could see, ahead of them, a greater river than they had ever before seen. They knew at once that this was the "father of waters" of the red men. You know, of course, that the wide, rushing stream was our Mississippi River. Joliet and Marquette pushed their canoes out into its waters and floated away to the south on the current.

The sacred calumet. The two white men and their

companions went down the Mississippi for miles and miles before they saw a single Indian. But at last they found some Indian villages not far from the west bank of the stream. The red people made a feast for the white visitors.

Every Indian, big and little, for miles around came to have a peep at the wonderful "palefaces." They had never before seen white people. By making signs Joliet and Marquette asked questions about the river and about the Indians who lived near it. Then they got into their canoes once more, ready to paddle on with the current.

Just before the canoes pushed away from the bank, the oldest chief among the red men came to Father Marquette with a gift. It was a stone pipe, the sacred calumet. The pipe was large and heavy. It had a long stem. The stem was cut in designs and painted and had around it a circle of red feathers.

The old chief "talked with his hands." He seemed to say to his new white friends, "Take the sacred calumet. Bad Indians will try to keep you from going down the river. Show them the pipe. They will let you pass."

After the canoes had gone down the river for many miles, the white men suddenly saw a great crowd of Indian warriors coming out across the water in their canoes. They were yelling and waving their heavy war clubs. The canoes of the Indians came close to those of the travelers. The warriors set arrows to the strings of

[185]

their bows. For a minute it looked as if the white men were to be killed.

Then Father Marquette remembered the sacred calumet. He stood up in his canoe and held the stone pipe above his head. What a change it brought! The warriors dropped their clubs and bows. Their fierce frowns changed into smiles. They took the white men to their village, gave them a feast, put food in the two canoes, and told the travelers all they knew about the dangerous places in the river.

With the help of the sacred calumet Joliet and Marquette went safely down the Mississippi as far as they cared to go. They learned that the big river empties its waters into the Gulf of Mexico. Then they turned their canoes about and started back to tell the French governor at Quebec about the success of their journey.

Why is the story of the journey of Joliet and Marquette called "Finding the Answer"?
Tell the story of the sacred calumet, or peace pipe.
The story says that "the warriors set arrows to the strings of their bows." What does that mean?
The old chief "talked with his hands," the story says. What is the meaning of that?

La Salle's Lost "Griffon"

A band of Indians once gathered on the bank of a river not far from Lake Erie. The red men were watching something that they did not understand at all. Near by a group of white men were cutting down trees and making planks and boards and putting them together to make a small ship. Small as the ship was, it was much larger than any boat or canoe the Indians had ever see

The red men were Iroquois Indians, and they did like to see these white men building this big "ca theirs in a part of the land the Indians claim own. But they did not worry much about clumsy craft that was being built. They wondered how in the world these foolish "palefaces" could ever paddle such a great, heavy monster as they were building.

But the warriors had a surprise in store for them. After a time they saw great squares of cloth rise above the white men's boat. What could those be for? Then the wonder of the red men rose still higher as they watched the great "canoe" move out into Lake Erie and away to the west without a man on board so much as touching a paddle.

The "Griffon." No wonder the Indians were surprised. They had just seen the first sailing ship that ever skimmed over the waters of our great northern lakes. It had been built for La Salle, one of the French leaders in America. He named his new ship the "Griffon."

La Salle had great plans about the forts and towns he wanted to begin along the lakes and rivers. He thought the "Griffon" would help him to carry on a good trade with the Indians. He sailed to Lake Michigan in his ship, loaded it with furs he bought from the Indians, and then ordered the captain of the "Griffon" to take the rich cargo to the fur market on the St. Lawrence River. Then La Salle and some of his men went down into Illinois and built a fort.

La Salle at last began to worry about his ship. A messenger had been ordered to come to him when the fur was sold. But no messenger came. The leader hurried away in a canoe to try to find out what had happened to the "Griffon."

What became of the "Griffon"? But the French people at Montreal had not heard a word about the ship. Not a man from the ship and not a beaver skin from her cargo had been seen at Montreal. La Salle hurried away to the Indians and asked them about the "Griffon." But none of the red men had seen a sign of the ship after it sailed out upon Lake Huron. Never again did La Salle see his ship or its captain and sailors. No one to this day knows what became of the "Griffon." Most people think it sank with all on board in some storm on the lake.

La Salle was sad, but he kept on with his plans. He traveled up and down the western lakes and rivers, and on one of his journeys found the mouth of the Mississippi River. He gave France a good claim to rich lands along the "Father of Waters."

Why did La Salle want to have a ship?

Tell about the surprise of the Indians when they saw the "Griffon" sail away.

Can you think of some other way the "Griffon" might have been lost?

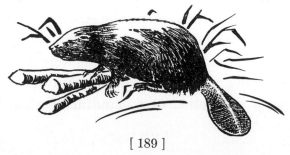

Pierre's Trade with the Indians

This is another story about Pierre, the French boy who lived for two years in a village of the Iroquois Indians.

When Pierre escaped from the Indians he went back to his home and friends in the French settlements. But he soon became restless and unhappy. He wanted to explore the lakes and forests which no white man had ever seen. He wanted to meet strange, new tribes of Indians and to trade with them for their furs.

At last Pierre and his brother-in-law, Medart, slipped away from the French towns in their canoe. In the canoe they had great bundles containing knives, brass kettles, little mirrors, beads, brass rings, hatchets, and cubes of red paint. Day after day the canoe skimmed on along the rivers and lakes until at last even Pierre was satisfied. When the two bold young Frenchmen went on shore, they found themselves among Indians who had never before seen white people.

Pierre and Medart built themselves a log house and then began to trade with the Indians. The simple red men did not know the value of the rich furs they wore or of those they captured along the streams. The things the white strangers had for sale in their log cabin seemed wonderful to Indian eyes. The warriors were ready to do almost anything in order to own a shiny steel knife, or a cube of red paint, or a handful of glass beads.

They eagerly brought to Pierre and Medart bundles of rich, heavy furs. Proudly they carried to their wigwams the articles they had received in trade with the "paleface" strangers.

Pierre and Medart spent three pleasant years among the simple, friendly red men. When they returned to the French settlements they had many canoes, and each canoe was piled high with bales of valuable furs.

Beaver skins were eagerly sought by the white men who traded with the Indians. The beaver fur was made into hats. Try to find out how these hats were made.

Beavers have sometimes been called "engineers." Why?

Can you tell why Pierre was well fitted to live and trade with the Indians?

Try to find pictures of beavers, minks, otters, and other fur-bearing animals.

Some of the people who left France and came to the French colony in America wanted to be farmers. Others came because they thought they could make money trading with the Indians. Still others wanted to explore the new land. But a number of Frenchmen who crossed the sea to America cared for none of these things. They wanted to help the Indians. They were religious teachers, or missionaries, and they wanted the red people of the forest to become Christians. The Indians called these missionaries "black gowns."

Father Jogues. You already know something about one of the missionaries. It was Father Marquette, you remember, who went down the Mississippi River with Joliet. Other "black gowns" lived among friendly Indians near the shores of Lake Huron. One of them was Father Jogues. The Indians liked Father Jogues, and many of them tried to live as he wished them to live. But the Iroquois warriors came and killed or drove away all the friendly Indians.

The Iroquois took Father Jogues to their village and there made him suffer. At last some white men helped him to escape from his enemies. But the leader of the missionaries ordered Father Jogues to go back to the cruel Iroquois and try to get them to become Christians.

Making Christians of the Iroquois warriors was a hard task for any one. But Father Jogues! He had run away from them once. That was something the warriors could not forgive.

The missionary knew all this, but he was like a good soldier. He went back, even though he was sure he would be killed. He tramped through the forest to the Iroquois village. There, a few days later, a huge Indian, lying in wait for the missionary, brought his war club down with terrible force on the head of Father Jogues.

Father Menard's "lost sheep." Father Menard was a feeble old missionary. When the Indians with whom he lived fled into the deep forest to escape their enemies, the old missionary thought that he ought to find them and go on telling them about the Christian religion. It was a long, hard journey. Besides, no one knew just where his red friends were. But he felt sure that God wanted him to find his "lost sheep," as he called them. So he started away in a canoe.

After many weeks Father Menard drew near to where he thought he would find his "lost sheep." One white man was with him in the canoe. The old man was so weak he could not help much with his paddle. He stepped out on the bank of the river so that the load in the canoe would not be so heavy. The other man paddled on a way, then waited. But Father Menard did not come. His companion hunted for him and shouted and fired his gun. But there was no answer. The poor old missionary was never seen again.

The missionaries among the Indians were brave and

true. They were cheerful and patient even though they did not get many of the Indians to change their ways and become Christians.

A. Three of the stories in this book have said something about missionaries. Can you write out these sentences, correctly filling the blanks?

Father _____ was a Spanish missionary who worked among the red men. A Christian worker from the English colonies was _____. Two of the French fathers who lived among the Indians were _____ and _____.

B. Match the words with the phrases that mean the same thing:

1. "black gown"   a. Indians who were cruel to the missionaries

2. Iroquois   b. Indians who hid in the forest

3. Father Jogues   c. A name that the Indians gave to some white men

4. Rene Menard   d. A missionary who was lost in the woods

5. "lost sheep"   e. A missionary killed by the Indians

Keeping the Friendship of the Red Men

The-Great-White-Father-Across-the-Sea. Most of the Indians liked the Frenchmen. The French traders and travelers often lived in the wigwams with the Indians. Sometimes the white men dressed like their red friends and took part in their dances. The Frenchmen called the Indians their children. They told the red

people about their king, the king of France. When they spoke of the king to the Indians they called him The-Great-White-Father-Across-the-Sea.

The fort on the "narrow waters." The Frenchmen knew that the Indians liked to make their journeys in their canoes. So Cadillac, a French leader, built a fort on a river between two of the largest lakes in all the western country. The Indians could travel to the new fort in their birch canoes.

Cadillac invited the red men to live near him. Some

of the warriors and their families traveled hundreds of miles to the fort and set up their wigwams just outside its log walls. They brought their furs and sold them to the white men living at the fort.

Cadillac built his fort in such a good place that soon a village grew up near by. Many Frenchmen lived there with their families. Some of them made their living by trading with the Indians, while others cleared the land and became farmers. All about the white people, in every direction, were the wigwams of the friendly Indians. Years later, after most of the Frenchmen and the Indians had moved away, what had been Cadillac's fort grew into the city of Detroit.

French towns in the warm South. One French leader followed the way La Salle had led down the Mississippi River. He found a place near the Gulf of Mexico where large rivers flow into a bay. Here he began a town. Down the rivers came the Indians to trade with the white men. The new village grew into the pleasant city of Mobile, Alabama.

Another leader among the French began a town which later became one of the most important cities in our country. This town was built on the "Father of Waters," not far from its mouth. French people from France and from different places in the New World moved to the new town on the Mississippi River. They liked the warm climate they found there. Large farms were begun near the town. Sugar cane was planted on

some of these farms. Soon sugar and molasses became important products. You probably have guessed, long before this, that the growing town on the great river was New Orleans.

A. Turn to the map on page 178. Find Detroit, Mobile, and New Orleans.

Plan to give a talk on this subject: "Why the French people got along so well with the Indians."

B. Answer these "why" questions.

1. Why were the Iroquois angry with the Frenchmen?
2. Why were the traders eager to buy beaver skins?
3. Why were the missionaries called by the red men "black gowns"?
4. Why did Cadillac build his fort where he did?
5. Why were the French eager to learn all they could about the Mississippi River?

C. Think before you answer these questions.
   1. Do you think that fur trading was as important as farming in making America what it is?
   2. Do you think the French people in America led more interesting lives than the English?
   3. Do you think it was a good thing for the Indians to be able to trade and get the beads and guns and hatchets of the white men?

D. What French leader
   began a colony?
   traded with the Indians?
   explored the Mississippi River?
   wanted to make Christians of the Indians?
   built the first ship to sail on the Great Lakes?

E. These stories about the French people and the Indians contain several new words and terms. Let's review some of them. Try telling the meanings of:
   "sacred calumet"   fort
   "pitched their wigwams"   war club
   "painted warriors"   the "lost sheep"
   "father of waters"

CHAPTER ELEVEN. WHO SHALL OWN THE NEWLY DISCOVERED LANDS?

NEMACOLIN'S PATH

Who was going to own the rivers and lakes and forests where the French people had built their forts and towns? In a way, of course, the Indians owned all the land. But as you have already seen, the white people did not often pay much attention to the red men's claims to the land they lived on. So the French said that all the western country along the Great Lakes and down the Mississippi River was theirs, because they were the first white people to explore it.

But the English people claimed the very lands which the French said belonged to them. The English said that the lands lying west of Massachusetts and Connecticut and Virginia were English lands. Of course, England and France could not both own the same piece of land at the same time. Year after year the quarrel over the western country became more bitter. The French and English people in America learned to hate each other

The "beautiful river." The French found a deep,

swift river flowing between high, forested banks. They called it "La Belle Riviere," which means, in English, the Beautiful River. We know it as the Ohio River. The French learned that this stream flowed into the Mississippi.

"Very well," said the Frenchmen "if we own the Mississippi River we own all the rivers that flow into it, and all the lands along all those streams."

One of the French leaders paddled down the Ohio River. A few white men and many Indians were with him. Every few miles the canoes drew to the bank of the river. There the men buried a lead plate. On each lead plate was a message which said that all the lands along the stream belonged to France. The messages were a warning to the English.

An Indian trail-blazer. At about this time a number of the men in Virginia decided to make an English settlement near the Ohio River. They gained what they thought were good rights to a large piece of land, and got ready to sell it to farmers who wanted to go into the new country to live. But how could the farmers go through the woods and over the mountains to the Ohio River without a road?

The men of Virginia could not think of any white man who would know where to place the new road. But they knew a friendly Indian of the Delaware tribe. This Indian's name was Nemacolin. When asked, Nemacolin said he would plan the road for the white men.

The Indian went to the very western edge of the settlements in Maryland. Then he started away into the forest, making marks on the trees to show where his road was to go. He crossed the rivers at the places where the water was not deep. He went over the mountains where they were lowest and easiest to climb. At last Nemacolin came to the Ohio River. Being an Indian, he had had no trouble in finding the best place for the white men's road. The "trace" he had made through the forest came to be known as "Nemacolin's Path."

Soon woodsmen went along the path making it into a rough road wide enough for a wagon. Later on parts of it became a smooth road over which settlers went with their wagons and families to the western lands.

Your book says that Nemacolin, being an Indian, had no trouble in finding the best place for the road. What does that mean?

Finish these sentences.
1. Nemacolin, an Indian, went into the woods to ____.
2. The French tried to warn the English away from the Ohio River by ____.
3. The French said the land along the Ohio River was theirs because ____.

George Washington, the Governor's Messenger

You can plainly see that the English and French were going to have trouble over the land along the Ohio River. The people of both England and France claimed it and were trying to move into it at the same time. The governor of Virginia decided to send a messenger to the French telling them to give up their forts and to go away.

The governor wondered whom he could send on such a dangerous journey. He needed someone who was brave and honest and would go straight to the French leaders with the message. But whoever went would need to know how to find his way through the woods without getting lost, and to camp by night in the wild country. At last the choice of the governor fell on George Washington, who was then twenty-one years of age. An

earlier story in the book tells why George Washington
was so well fitted to carry the governor's message.

Soon the young messenger was on his way through the
deep woods. With him were one or two companions. They
waded through the rivers and climbed over steep mountains. Day after day they went on until they had crossed
much of the wild country in the western part of
Pennsylvania. At last the men arrived at the French
forts.

The French soldiers treated Washington kindly. But
they only shook their heads at the message. They said
they had been ordered to build the forts, and there they
would stay until their ruler, the King of France, gave
them fresh commands. There was nothing for George

Washington to do but to start on the long journey back to Virginia.

Many dangers came to the governor's messenger as he journeyed on toward home. Once an Indian shot at him with his flintlock gun. Once he was swept away in the icy current of a broad river. If he had not been a good swimmer he would have drowned. He reached an island in the river, wet and shivering, and at last was able to go on with his journey.

He was glad when he finally reached his Virginia home. The governor had only words of the warmest praise for his young messenger.

What journey was George Washington asked to make?
Why did the governor of Virginia need a messenger?
Why was the journey of Washington a hard and dangerous one?

White Soldiers and Red Warriors

When the French leaders refused to leave their forts, the English decided to try driving them away. An army of England's red-coated soldiers marched through the woods toward the French forts. George Washington and a number of the colonial soldiers went to fight beside the soldiers of England.

Fighting the Indians. Great numbers of the Indians decided to help their friends, the French. They came in their canoes to the largest of the French forts. When the English army drew near the fort, the Indians and the French soldiers hurried out and drove their enemies back through the forest. Great numbers of the English soldiers lost their lives in the terrible fight.

The people in England and in the English colonies were worried. But at this time England had a great leader. His name was William Pitt. Pitt would not give up. He sent new armies to America from England. One of these armies marched through the woods toward the strong French fort on the Ohio River.

How Pittsburgh got its name. The leader of this second army that was sent to capture the French fort was General Forbes. He was an old man. He had a disease from which he was slowly dying. But when the soldiers wanted to turn back, General Forbes ordered them to keep on toward the fort. In order to go with his men the sick general rode in a litter, or hammock, between two horses. He knew that William Pitt would want him to go on, no matter how sick he was.

Soon the general and his soldiers drew close to the great French fort. The men had their guns ready. They expected at every moment to hear the wild yells of the Indian warriors. They were sure they were going to have a great battle.

Imagine their surprise and joy when, peering out of the forest, they saw only the burned, black ruins of what had once been the fort. The French and the Indians had been even more scared of the English soldiers than the English had been of them. They had set their fort on fire and had hurried away out of danger.

That was the end of the French along the Ohio River. After that the English owned all the land in that part of the country.

The French fort had stood at a place where two streams come together to make the Ohio River. The spot was a good place for a fort, so the English built a new fort there, and named it Fort Pitt, in honor of the English leader, William Pitt.

The point of land between the two rivers was a good place for a town as well as for a fort. Soon a growing village stood there. After our country, the United States, was born, the village grew to be a great city— only under a new name: Pittsburgh.

The Indians seemed to like the Frenchmen better than they liked the Englishmen. Can you tell why?

On a map of Pennsylvania find the city of Pittsburgh. Why was Pittsburgh an important place to build a fort?

Try to draw a picture of the French fort. Remember, it was made of logs. Find and study a picture of the flag of France; then put a French flag on a staff above the fort.

THE ACADIANS ARE CARRIED AWAY

Numbers of the French settlers who came to America made their homes near the St. Lawrence River. But the earliest of all the French farmers in the new northern colony of France lived near the Atlantic Ocean. Some of them arrived in the New World even before Captain

John Smith and the other Englishmen with him began the settlement at Jamestown. They called the place where they made their farms Acadia. They were known as the Acadians.

In an early war between England and France the English soldiers won some important victories. When the war ended the Acadians found that their country no longer belonged to France but to England. So the Acadians, who had at first been subjects of the French king, now became the subjects of the king of England.

Trying to make Frenchmen into Englishmen. The Acadians were simple people. They did not understand

what the war had been about. All they knew was that they did not want to try to become Englishmen. They wanted to go on being French people under the French king. When they were asked to swear to be loyal to their new king they refused. They went on caring for their herds of cattle and tending their small farms just as they had always done. They did not like the English people. They did not want to have anything to do with them. Again and again they refused to promise to be loyal.

The coming of the soldiers. For a long time the English rulers were patient with the Acadians. But when the new war began in the valley of the Ohio River it soon spread to other parts of America, and to the old lands in Europe as well. The English leaders were afraid that the Acadians might help the French in the great war which had begun. They decided to prevent this.

Not long after the war had begun, English ships and English soldiers came to the Acadian country. Soon the Acadian men working in the fields received a command from the leader of the soldiers. They were told that they must drop their work and gather in their churches. They did not dare to disobey the soldiers. They crowded into their churches. All about them were the soldiers with their guns and their shining bayonets.

On the English ships. The poor French farmers could hardly believe their ears when they heard what was going to happen. They learned that the soldiers were going to force them on board the ships and have them carried away to strange lands. They could not believe, at first, that anyone would be cruel enough to drag them away from their little white houses, their farms, and their herds. But it was so.

Hundreds of the frightened Acadian families ran away into the woods where the soldiers could not find them. But six thousand of the people were forced on board the ships. They were carried away on the ocean.

Some of the ships went to Boston and New York, while others sailed south to Charleston and Savannah. At all of those places Acadians were taken from the ships and made to live among the English colonists. They were lonesome and unhappy. They had lost everything they had once owned.

Not many of the Acadian farmers and their families ever got back to their pleasant land. Many of them, when the chance came, went down to Louisiana, where other French people lived, and there built new homes. Some time you will have a chance to read a fine poem, called "Evangeline," which tells the story of the Acadians.

Why did the English leaders want to send the Acadians away?

Perhaps you could make a play from this story of the Acadians. In your first scene the Acadians could be talking about the war. Let their words show how they felt about the English. What would your second scene be about? And the third? If you make a real play out of the story you will have to decide how the Acadians dressed, and what kind of uniforms were worn by the English officers. Think about that.

Two Heroes

England and France started to fight each other over who owned the lands near the Ohio River. But in the long war that followed they were really struggling for all the country in the north and along the Mississippi River.

The French had a strong fort at Quebec. It was on a rock high above the St. Lawrence River. In command of the French soldiers who were guarding Quebec was General Montcalm. He was one of the best French leaders in America. He knew that if the English took the fort at Quebec from him the French would lose a great deal of their land in America. He tried to place his soldiers so that they could guard Quebec closely day and night.

An English army came to attack Montcalm's soldiers and try to capture Quebec. But how could the English soldiers climb up the steep river bank, and then up the

rocks to the walls of the fort? General Wolfe, who commanded the English soldiers, at last saw a narrow path leading up from the river. In the night his men crept up this path. When daylight came the English soldiers were in line, ready for battle.

General Montcalm was surprised when he saw Wolfe's soldiers on the plain so near Quebec. He led his army out to the fight. But the French soldiers got the worst of the battle and fled back inside the walls of Quebec.

Soon they gave up the city and the fort to the English.

In the battle for Quebec General Wolfe was struck by flying bullets and fell dying among his soldiers. General Montcalm was also wounded and had to be carried back to the fort. In a short time both generals were dead. Many years later a monument was built to the memory of these two brave enemies. On one side of the monument is the name of the English general who won the battle, and on another that of the French general who lost it.

A. Finish these sentences.
_____ was the leader on the English side.
The French general was _____.
Both lost their lives in the battle at _____.

B. Do you like the idea of one monument to two soldiers who had to be enemies in war?

WINNERS AND LOSERS

Just as Montcalm had feared, after the English got Quebec they soon took all the other French forts and lands. The king of France had nothing at all left of his great possessions in North America except two small islands. England owned all the rest, all the way to the Mississippi River, and north to the Arctic Ocean.

The French people in the small towns along the St. Lawrence River and in the villages farther to the west were sad when they saw the French flags taken down from above all the forts and saw the French soldiers go aboard the ships and sail away for France. Of course, not many of the French people could follow the soldiers back to France. They were too poor. They had to stay where they were and try to get used to the idea of being subjects of the king of England.

How the Indians felt. The red friends of France were puzzled and angry over the way the war turned out. They had felt sure that their French "fathers" would always live in the little western forts, trading with them for their beaver skins. They did not know what to think when they saw the French soldiers go away and the red-coated men of England come to take their places.

Pontiac, an Indian leader. One Indian warrior did not trust these new "palefaces" who had come. He did not think they would be fair and just to the red people. He made plans to have the warriors all band together and try to drive the white people away from the lands where the Indians lived. This warrior's name was Pontiac.

Pontiac traveled from wigwam to wigwam talking to the fighting men of all the tribes. The warriors agreed to start a war against the white men. On a certain day set by Pontiac the Indians rushed upon the small forts where the English soldiers lived. Many of the forts were taken by the Indians. Often every soldier in these forts was killed.

But in some of the forts the white soldiers would not surrender. Other soldiers came to help them and to build new forts where older forts had been burned by

the warriors. At last the Indians became tired of the fighting and went back to their hunting and fishing. The English people stayed in the country, and some of them began trading with the Indians. After that the English soldiers and the red warriors got along well together.

A. Answer these "why" questions.
1. Why did the French people in America feel sad over the way the war turned out?
2. Why were the Indians puzzled and unhappy?
3. Why did Pontiac plan a war against the English soldiers?
4. Why did the English and the Indians at last become friends?

B. Choose the right ending for each sentence.
   1. The Acadians were carried off to (England, the English colonies).
   2. George Washington went as a messenger to the (French, Indians).
   3. The strongest French fort was at (Montreal, New Orleans, Boston, Quebec).
   4. When the war was over Quebec and Detroit and the near-by lands belonged to (Holland, England, Spain, France).
   5. The Indians living in the west (helped the English against the French, did not help either side, were sorry that the English had won the war).

C. Match each word with the right sentence.
   1. Wolfe   a. He planned a road for English settlers to follow.
   2. Nemacolin   b. He went to warn the French to go away.
   3. Montcalm   c. He was a "black gown."
   4. Jogues   d. He was a French leader who lost his life in war.
   5. Washington   e. He captured Quebec from the French.

V. CHANGE AND GROWTH IN OUR AMERICA

CHAPTER TWELVE. HOW AMERICA BECAME A BETTER PLACE TO LIVE

TRAVELING IN A STAGE COACH

America did not stay as wild and rough a country as it was in the times of the Pilgrim Fathers. Farms took the place of woods. The old Indian trails were made wider for use as roads.

After the roads had been made better, the people in America began to travel about in wagons and carriages. Sometimes they used two-wheeled carts. A light carriage was the chaise, drawn by one horse. Americans soon began calling the chaise a "shay." Perhaps you have heard about the "one-hoss shay." Then there was a heavy carriage, often drawn by four horses, called a chariot. Rich people rode to church in their chariots.

After a number of years stage coaches were to be seen on some of the best roads. The men who owned the stage coaches charged a fare for riding in their coaches.

If you had been living in those days, and wanted to

make a trip in a stage coach, you would need to get up very early, for the coaches started out at three o'clock in the morning. In your coach there is room for nine passengers and the driver. If you have any bags or satchels, you will need to hold them in your lap or put them under your feet.

You will soon learn that there are many rocks and stumps in the road and that there are no springs under your coach. You will need to hang on for dear life if you expect to stay in your seat. If the coach gets into a deep mud hole the driver may ask you and the other pas-

sengers to get out and push. When you come to streams, the horses will splash right through them, for there are no bridges. You will cross the wider, deeper rivers on a big raft.

Eighteen hours is a day's travel on a stage coach. So you will finish your day's ride at about nine o'clock at night. Long before daylight the next morning the driver's horn will sound, warning you to get up in a hurry and get ready for another long, bumpy journey.

Do you wonder that so few people traveled about in the America of long ago?

Try writing a story about a trip in a stage coach. Why not illustrate your story with some pictures drawn by yourself? Put a tavern (hotel) with its sign at the top of your paper, and a drawing of a stage coach at the bottom.

Have you any money in your pocket or your purse? A penny? A nickel? A dime? Or even a quarter, perhaps? And have you used any money today to buy something you wanted?

The children of our early America would have been greatly surprised at such questions. Of course they didn't have any money! Even father and mother were without any money, real money, much of the time. Would it not seem odd to live in a home without money, in a town without money? It did not seem very odd then. People did not need money as much as we do. As you know, nearly everything that was needed was made or raised right at home. The people did not need to do much shopping.

When the towns and villages grew older and larger, the people had a greater need for money. More articles were bought and sold than in earlier days, and money is always needed where there is trade. But all through the colonies most families got along with very little money.

Kinds of money. The Indians used wampum for money. "Wampum" was their word for strings of small shells. Shells of different colors had different values. Some of the white men, because they had nothing better, used the Indian wampum for money.

In Virginia tobacco was money. Some of the first

settlers there planned to marry girls who had been sent over to the colony. But before the marriage could take place the man had to pay the cost of the bride's voyage across the ocean. He paid this cost with tobacco.

Beaver skins were often used as money. Other kinds of colonial "money" were soap, rice, corn, turkeys, and bullets.

A story about real money. Of course, none of the articles that have been mentioned was handy to use as money. So the colony of Massachusetts planned to make some real money. The governor found a man who knew how to coin metal pieces of money. The new coins this man made had a picture of a pine tree stamped on one side. They were always called "pine tree shillings."

There is a story about Captain John Hall, the man who made the pine tree shillings. The captain took pay for his work in the new shillings. At last he had a great store of them.

One day a young man, Samuel Sewell by name, came to Captain Hall to ask the captain for his daughter's hand in marriage. Captain Hall asked his daughter, who was a very plump girl, to stand on a scale. Then a great trunk was dragged into the room. It was full of pine tree shillings. These were poured into the other pan on the scale until the girl's end of the scale came up.

"There, Samuel!" cried the maker of coins, "you shall have my daughter as your wife, and her weight in pine tree shillings besides."

A. If you have a coin collection, this would be a good time to show it to your classmates.

B. Match these:
   1. coin   a. string of small shells
   2. wampum   b. a metal piece of money
   3. pine tree shilling c. a coin used in Massachusetts

CARRYING THE MAIL

It would seem strange to us to write a letter and then be obliged to plan how we were going to send our letter where we wanted it to go. In early times everyone who wrote a letter had to puzzle over this. Most poor people settled the matter by not writing letters. The rich ones sent the few letters they wrote by special messengers.

The need for post offices and for men to carry the mail became so great that the leading men of Massachusetts colony decided to do something about it. They asked the rulers of the colony to start a regular way of carrying the mail. The rulers agreed, and said they would find "some mete person to take in and convey letters according to directions." John Hayward got the job. He was the first mail man in our country.

Carrying the mail on horseback. Virginia was the next colony to have men to carry the mail. To keep the men from becoming careless and losing the mail, it was agreed that every time one of the mail men lost a letter he had to pay a fine of one hogshead of tobacco.

Soon men riding good horses began to carry letters

between the towns of New York and Boston. There was one locked mail box in each place. People dropped their letters in these boxes much as we do. On Monday morning the mail man took them, put them in his saddlebags, and began his long journey. In about two weeks a letter mailed in New York would reach the person it was meant for in Boston.

Benjamin Franklin and the mail. After a time the mail was carried by the stages instead of by men on horseback. Benjamin Franklin had charge of the mail for all the colonies. He traveled about to see how well the work of carrying the mail was being done. When our new nation, the United States, was being formed, Benjamin Franklin went on with his work of caring for the mail in America.

Find the meaning of the word "mete" used here. It is an old-fashioned word.

What do the words "to pay a fine" mean?

This is a good place for a "Then and Now" chart. See how many differences you can think of between taking care of the mail in early times and today. Rule a paper like this and then begin:

	Then	Now
how the mail was carried		
the time it took		

(Think of other points.)

Making Hats and Clothing

People did not go to work in factories in colonial times, for there were no factories. But numbers of skilled persons were busy making useful articles in their homes or in small shops.

You already know about the spinning and weaving done by the women and girls in their homes. From the flax raised on the farms they could make linen cloth. They knew how to weave woolen cloth, too.

At first there were few sheep in the colonies to furnish the wool. Often the people in America wrote letters about this to their friends in England. When they heard that friends were planning to cross the ocean to

America, the settlers told them in their letters to bring sheep with them. So it happened that often, when a vessel came to Plymouth or Boston or some other town, a few sheep would be brought from the deck of the ship to the wharf.

After a few years many sheep were to be seen on the colonial farms. The women learned to make as fine woolen cloth as that being made in England.

Most of the beaver skins bought by the traders from the Indians went into the making of beaver hats. Those fine hats, which were worn by so many of the men in both America and Europe, were made in a great number of small shops in the colonial towns and cities. The hat makers became skilled in heating and pressing mats of beaver fur, in cutting the mats into the right shapes, and in shaping the broad-rimmed hats of that time. The beaver hats made in America were sold in many parts of the world.

In quite early times the hat makers left the rims down. If you can find pictures of the early Puritan men, you will see them wearing hats in that fashion. But later the rims were turned up on three sides and fastened to the crown with pins or buckles. Such men as George

Washington and Benjamin Franklin wore their beaver hats with the rims fastened up, as pictures of them will show.

It might be interesting to illustrate this story with pictures of hats.

This story says there were no factories in the colonies. It states that articles were made in small shops. How is a shop different from a factory?

From this list choose the things the colonial people used in making the things they wore:

silk	beaver **fur**
flax	rubber
wool	rayon
leather	

Living in a Colonial City

The cities of early America did not grow very fast or become very large. Yet a number of them grew into important towns. A traveler said this about New York City two hundred years ago:

"The city is one mile long and half a mile wide. The streets are paved with round pebbles. Most of the houses are made of bricks, and have tile roofs. The people of New York are of many races."

Early America's greatest town. Philadelphia, the town where Benjamin Franklin lived, was the finest town of colonial times. When William Penn began the city, he laid out broad streets. The streets crossed each other dividing the town into squares like the squares on a checker board.

Some of the houses in Philadelphia were three stories high. The best streets were paved with round stones, called cobblestones, while the sidewalks were laid with bricks.

Benjamin Franklin liked this city where he lived. If we could have visited this wise, friendly man, he would have been proud to show us about the town. He would have taken us to see the free hospital—something almost no other city in the whole world had at that time. Then there was the library where a person could draw out books very much as we do today. That, too, was a

new idea. Franklin started both the hospital and the library of Philadelphia.

Lighting streets and putting out fires. If there had been a fire while we were visiting in Philadelphia we should have seen a "bucket brigade" passing pails of water from hand to hand in the direction of the fire. In Philadelphia the men of the "brigade" knew their places in the line and got to them quickly. Their leaders were skilled fire fighters.

If we had gone out on the streets at night, we should have noticed the street lights. They were only whale-oil lamps, and the light they gave was dim, but they were much better than nothing. Not many other cities of that time were so well lighted as Philadelphia.

What did William Penn do to make Philadelphia a pleasant town?

In what ways did Benjamin Franklin make it a still better city?

Not many books were to be found in the homes of long-ago America. There were so few books that men and women, boys and girls, read what they had very carefully. Often they read them over and over and almost learned them by heart.

Books for children. After a number of years a few books for boys and girls found their way into the colonial homes. These were odd little books. They tried to teach their readers something in spelling or arithmetic, or, perhaps, tried to give hints about having good habits or being good. One such book had in it a number of rhymes like this:

> J was a jay
>   that prattles and toys;
> K was a key
>   that locked up bad boys.

Poor Richard's Almanac. Benjamin Franklin and some of the other printers made almanacs each year and sold them to the people. The almanacs were paper-covered books that told the farmers how to manage their farms. They contained many wise sayings. Franklin's *Poor Richard's Almanac* was eagerly read in Europe as well as in colonial homes.

"The sleeping fox catches no chickens," warned Poor Richard.

Another almanac had this rhyme about the coming of winter:

> Ladies take heed:
> Lay down your fans,
> And handle well
> Your warming pans.

The small newspapers of those times were printed once a week. In them there was very little news, but the people were glad to read them.

Make as long a list as you can of the ways we have of learning the news.

Perhaps you will begin with newspapers and telephones. Then put a check mark after all the ways in your list that the colonial people also had for getting the news.

Why not make a "Then" and "Now" chart for newspapers? Start like this:

	Then	*Now*
How often printed	weekly	daily

A LITTLE JOURNEY IN THE SOUTH

If you had lived when George Washington was a boy, and had wanted to make a journey in the South, you might have traveled on horseback. Not many good roads for wagons or carriages had been made in the southern colonies.

One thing you would have noticed as you rode across Virginia was the fine big house each plantation owner had built for himself and his family. Like George

Washington's Mount Vernon home, many of the other good houses looked out over a broad river. At the rear of the houses you would have noticed the many small cabins where the slave families lived.

You would also have seen small homes and small farms in Virginia and the other southern colonies. The people who lived in such places did not own any slaves.

As you traveled along you would not have seen many towns. You would often have wondered if you could find a hotel where you could spend the night.

If your journey took you to Charleston, South Carolina, you would have found that town to be a gay and pleasant little city. The owners of the great farms had homes in Charleston. They and their families and neighbors had many grand parties and dances. At such times the suits worn by the men and the dresses of the women were as costly as those of the rich people of England.

Name the English colonies that were in the South.

Give the names of three things raised on the southern plantations.

Some Old Laws and Customs That We Should Not Like

England made some laws for her colonies that the people in America did not like. We should not like them, either. One law said that the tobacco raised in America could be sent away only to the markets in England.

In another law it was ordered that the colonial people could buy certain things only in England.

In colonial times the rulers had strange ideas about punishing persons who did not obey the law. Such persons were cruelly punished, often in public places where everyone could see what was going on. Persons who did wrong were often tied to whipping posts and, while people looked on, were lashed until their backs were wet with blood. Sometimes the person who had broken a law had to stand with his hands and head pushed through holes in a plank and fastened there. In some towns there was a ducking stool. The person who was being punished was fastened to the stool, and then the stool was let down into the water.

You have already read about the prisons in England

for men who did not pay their debts. America, also, had jails where people were put when they could not pay their debts. The jails were dark, dirty places. In them the most wicked men and the poor people who had done nothing worse than to owe money they could not pay were all thrown together. Slowly America gave up the cruel laws and punishments of early times.

Can you think of any reason why it was once thought best to punish persons who did wrong where everyone could look on?

Here is a good missing-word test for you.

1. Most early homes in America were built of ____. They were heated by means of ____. At night the light was supplied by ____, ____, and ____.
2. Later on colonial houses were built of ____ or ____.
3. A famous early schoolbook was ____. Another book used in school was called ____. The ____ was a book found in nearly all of the homes of the Puritans.
4. Three ways to travel about in early America were ____, ____, and ____.
5. A group of settlements under one governor was called a ____.
6. Some of the first coins made in America were ____.
7. A valuable product obtained from the Indians was ____. Two products obtained by the fishermen were ____ and ____. A product raised in swamps in the South was ____.
8. The colony where many debtors settled was ____. The Quakers went to ____. Dutch traders first settled in ____. The colony begun by the Puritans was ____. The first English settlers went to ____.

CHAPTER THIRTEEN. STORIES ABOUT PIONEERS

Daniel Boone, the Hunter

Daniel Boone lived at the edge of the wild country where the forest trees stood tall and straight and close together. Boone liked to go hunting, for in the woods were deer, bears, wolves, and flocks of wild turkeys. On his hunting trips he dressed much like an Indian. He wore a coon-skin cap. He carried a long rifle. Boone was tall and straight, and his sharp eyes took in everything there was to see. In the woods he slipped along as silently as any red hunter.

Off to the west of his log cabin Daniel Boone could see mountains. When he climbed the nearest ones he could see still more mountains beyond them. An old hunter told Daniel about the wonderful game country west of the last of the mountains. After that the young hunter could think of nothing but the new country beyond the hills. He dreamed about the great elks that went bounding through the tall grass and about the buffaloes that crowded down to the streams to drink. He lost interest in the woods near his home. He wanted to wander in the wild land across the mountains.

At last Daniel Boone and five companions tramped away into the mountains. For five weeks they scrambled over the steep hills, picked their way through the dark woods, and waded or swam the swift rivers.

At last they came out into a fair country where the groves of trees looked like little parks, and where the open places were covered with rich, tall grass. Here and there the hunters found springs bubbling up out of the ground. Where the waters of these springs touched the rocks and soil, they left a faint taste of salt.

The hoofed wild animals love salt. Each bubbling spring was a "salt lick" where the animals came and licked the salt. Never before had Daniel Boone seen so many wild animals. He was in the land he had dreamed about. Already the beautiful, wild country was called Kentucky.

The Indians hunted in Kentucky, too. They killed one

of Boone's companions and scared some of the others away. Boone's brother went back home to get supplies. So Daniel Boone was alone in the wild land. But the great hunter did not care. He liked being alone in the woods. He was happy, even though he was without salt, sugar, and flour, and without even a dog for a companion.

Boone had to be very careful. Always bands of Indians were roving about. They did not like to have the white men in their hunting grounds. When he built a fire to cook his meals he used only pieces of wood that made no smoke that keen Indian eyes might see at a distance. His supper he ate early, while it was still light. Then he tramped away silently into the woods to lie down at last and sleep miles from his dying camp fire.

The Indians could not capture the hunter Daniel Boone.

After two years in Kentucky Daniel Boone made his way back over the mountains to his log house in North Carolina.

Try to draw a picture of Daniel Boone. Make him tall and very straight. Put a coon-skin cap on his head. The black-and-white striped coon's tail should be shown hanging down behind. Why not have the hunter standing on a mountain looking at something in the distance?

Choose from this list some words that describe Daniel Boone.

daring	strong	straight
weak	good hunter	afraid
tall	short	had sharp eyes

DANIEL BOONE'S FORT

After Boone got back home he kept thinking about Kentucky. He wanted to take his family and friends with him and go there to live. His two years in the new country had told him that the Indians, although they hunted in Kentucky, did not live there. When he heard that some of the tribes had given up their claims to Kentucky, even as a hunting ground, he made ready to go there to settle.

First, Boone took men with him and made a trail over the mountains. It was not a wide trail, and wagons could not pass over it. But it went through the rough country the easiest way. Horses with packs on their backs could follow it. The new trail was soon called Boone's Wilderness Road.

In a short time the hunter and his companions reached the banks of the Kentucky River. Here the men found a smooth piece of ground and began to build a fort.

The men first cut down trees, trimmed off the branches, and sharpened the tree trunks at one end. Then they set the sharpened logs on end close together. The logs made a high, strong fence, which was placed around a piece of ground about half as big as a city block. The fence, or stockade, had two strong gates in it, one on either side. The gates could be fastened shut by means of strong oak bars.

Next the men went to work building cabins. They built the small log houses along the sides of the fence, on the inside. The doors of the houses opened out into the closed space. So the fort was really a village as well as a fort. It was also a sort of barnyard, for the cattle and horses the people brought to Kentucky could be brought inside the walls of the fort whenever there was danger from the Indians. The people named the new fort Boonesboro.

At last Boonesboro was ready for the wives and children of the settlers. Boone went back to North Carolina and got his wife and children. Mrs. Boone and her daughter were the first white women to go over the Wilderness Road into Kentucky.

Do you think you could make a trail through the woods? How would you do it? Would you cut down the big trees along the way?

Tell how Boone and his men built Boonesboro.

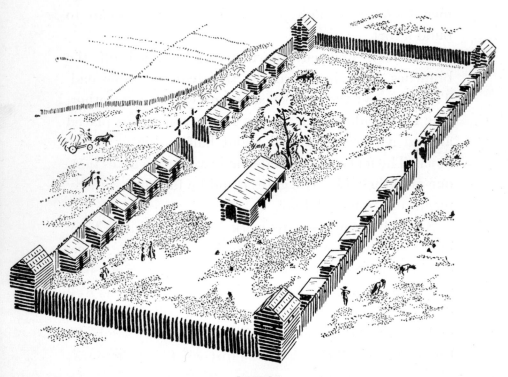

Little Rachel Donelson lived with her parents in a log house in the mountains of North Carolina. A swift river ran past their house. On the banks of this river, and along other streams that flowed through the mountain valleys, lived the friends and neighbors of the Donelsons. Nearly every bit of furniture in the small houses was home-made. The clothing of the men and women and children was like that of the Indians, or, if made of cloth, it was cloth that had been woven in the log cabins.

One day the leader of the settlers came back from a long trip in the western woods. His name was James Robertson. He said he had found a still better place for the settlers to live. John Donelson, Rachel's father, and a number of the other men decided to go with James Robertson to the new land. Of course that meant that the women and children would go, too.

Making plans and getting started on the journey. One morning a long line of horses started up the mountain path with heavy packs on their backs. With the horses went a band of men, their rifles ready. James Robertson was at their head.

But the Donelson family, and many other families, went down to the bank of the largest river. There a number of big, flat-bottomed boats were waiting for them. Already some of the boats were piled high with

bags of corn, rolls of blankets, strong boxes, and spinning wheels. In some of the boats were crates of chickens. The people all crowded on board the boats, Rachel and her mother finding a place near the middle of one of them. John Donelson was captain of all the boats. Soon the loaded boats were all floating swiftly down the river.

Down the Tennessee River. What a dangerous journey that was! Sometimes the boats stuck in the sand and

mud and had to be pushed off into deeper water. Now
and then a boat was almost wrecked in the swift current.
More than once Rachel shut her eyes tight and held to
the sides of the boat as it swept down among the black
rocks in the river.

A terrible thing happened on one of the boats. One of

[243]

the passengers came down with smallpox. This boat stayed far behind the others to keep the disease from spreading to the other boats. Indians, hiding on the river bank, rushed down on this boat and killed the people on it. Smallpox then spread among the Indians and many of them died.

The boats floated for miles and miles down the Tennessee River. At last they came to the Ohio River. Up the Ohio River Captain Donelson and his men pushed the boats, and then up the Cumberland River. It was hard work now, for the current was against the boats, not with them. To the women and children it began to seem as if that journey would never end.

At last the boats came in sight of rolling hills along the river. Among the hills there were good springs of sparkling water. Best of all, there on the bank of the river, waiting for the travelers, stood James Robertson and his men. They had already built a good, strong fort where all would be safe from the Indians.

The wooden fort which now became Rachel Donelson's home was called Nashboro. The fort grew into a town, and the town changed its name. It became the city of Nashville, Tennessee.

And little Rachel? She grew up and became the wife of Tennessee's greatest hero, Andrew Jackson, the seventh president of the United States.

For the girls: Pretend that you are Rachel Donelson. Keep a diary of your voyage down the river.

For the boys: Tell the class about experiences you have had out in a boat on a lake or stream.

Draw a picture showing a boat like one you think the settlers used. Remember, it must be large and strong.

How the Women and Girls Fooled
the Indians

The Boones and their friends soon had neighbors in Kentucky. A number of little forts, much like Boonesboro, were built. The families of the settlers lived in the forts and raised corn and vegetables on the rich soil outside.

One morning some of the men hurried in to one of these forts with bad news. They had just seen a large number of Indians in all their war paint creeping through the bushes toward the fort. As soon as all the people were inside, the big gates of the fort were shut and fastened.

Something to worry about. The men in the fort knew that its log walls were strong. They knew they could shoot straight with their long rifles if the Indians rushed at the fort. But there was one thing that worried everyone in the fort. Inside the walls there was no well or spring, and the water barrels and water pails were already almost empty. What if the Indians waited about for several days? How could the people in the fort live without water to drink? They just had to get a good supply of water. But how—with the Indians hiding in

the grass and bushes all around the fort? Then one of the women spoke up:

"I know how to get the water. Give the pails and kettles to us women. Yes, and to the big girls, too. Then open the gate."

"But the Indians!" cried one of the men. "They will be hiding near the spring—trust them to be cunning enough for that! They will leap out and kill you all."

"No, they won't," the pioneer woman answered. "They think they've surrounded the fort without our knowing it. They expect to surprise us, kill us all, and burn the fort. Well, then, when they see us women and girls going after water they'll be sure we don't know there's an Indian within fifty miles. They'll leave us alone. They think that if they attack us they'll lose their chance to surprise the fort."

A dangerous errand. The men saw the truth in the brave woman's words. In a minute the gate nearest the spring opened wide. Out marched the women and girls, carrying empty vessels in each hand.

"Now mind you!" whispered their leader. "Not a look into the bushes. Laugh and talk just as if there wasn't anything around bigger than a squirrel to be scared of."

Do you think it was easy to walk to the spring, and act gay and happy, and not look for the war feathers and the beady black eyes of an Indian warrior behind every bush? Especially when you knew that not one Indian, but many of them, were there, watching every move that was made, ready to jump out and kill?

It turned out just as the leader of the women said it

would. The Indians watched them fill their pails, but the warriors lay hidden and made no move. The women and girls walked slowly back along the path to the gate. Not until they were safe through the big gate, and a shout of relief went up from the watching men, did the red warriors realize that they had been fooled.

Try making a little play out of this story. One boy could be the settler who first saw the Indians. A group of boys could be the Indians in hiding. Others could be the men watching in the fort. Of course most of the girls will want to "go to the spring for water."

Why not change the story, putting in more talking than there is in the book?

A New Use for Tobacco

This is another story about Daniel Boone.

Some of the Indians learned to know the great hunter quite well. They admired him. They thought it wonderful that a "paleface" could be as clever in the woods as they were. They feared him, but they liked him at the same time.

One day four Cherokee Indians decided to capture Boone and take him away with them. They crept up to where he was working, alone, taking care of some tobacco he had raised.

Boone had a shed where he put his tobacco to dry. A part of the crop was already well dried. The white man was standing on some poles up near the top of his shed. He was lifting the dry tobacco plants up to a platform still nearer the peak. All at once he heard his name in broken English. He looked down, and there stood the four Cherokees. They were grinning up at him. But they also had their guns pointing at him.

"We know you, Boone. We got you this time. You no get away," one of the Cherokees said, in the queer, grunting way the Indians had when speaking.

Daniel Boone did not act the least bit surprised. He noticed that the warriors stood right in the door of his shed. They had him trapped. He knew he would have to use his head this time.

"Hello, friends," he cried, smiling down at the warriors. He acted as if he were glad to see his visitors. "Yes, I'll be glad to go along with you. Just let me finish putting this tobacco up."

All the time Boone was talking he was gathering up the dry tobacco. The Indians, down below on the ground, were looking up at him. Suddenly the white man threw his bundle of tobacco right into the coppery faces. Then he jumped down among the red men.

That dry, powdery tobacco! It got into the Indians' eyes and noses. They began to cough and sneeze and choke. They were blinded by the stinging tobacco dust. When Boone bounced down among them they reached for him, tripped over each other, and fell in a tangled heap.

Long before the Cherokees were again able to see well

enough to aim a gun, Daniel Boone was safe inside his cabin, his own gun in his hands. He could have shot the Indians, but he laughed to himself and let them go.

This is a good story to tell. Tell it to someone at home. Try to make your story exciting and interesting.

How do you suppose these Cherokee Indians got guns?

The "White Indian"

The people in the little forts in Kentucky and Tennessee had to do without many things. Sometimes they did not even have salt for their food. They could not often make the long journey back to the older settlements for a supply of salt. Now and then parties of men went to one of the salt springs and there made their own salt.

Daniel Boone once went with some of his men to the salt spring on the Licking River to make salt. While the leader hunted and supplied the men with meat, they began making salt.

One morning Boone was following the track of a deer far from the salt lick. All at once a hundred Indians came out of the forest. They saw the hunter and dashed toward him. Boone turned and bounded away. He was a good runner, but some of the young warriors were even better. They caught the white man and made him a prisoner. Then they captured the salt makers and hurried away to their village in Ohio.

Making Daniel Boone into an Indian. The Indians

were proud of their great band of prisoners. But they were proudest of all at the thought that the great hunter, Daniel Boone, had at last been captured. They took him to the English fort at Detroit and showed him to the commander there. But when an Englishman tried to buy Boone from them in order to set him free, the warriors shook their heads. Daniel Boone was not for sale. They took him back to their village. It was their plan to make him a warrior.

First the Indians pulled the hairs out of Boone's head, leaving only a thick bunch on top. This was the "scalp lock." All warriors wore their hair that way. This part of being made into an Indian must have hurt. Then Boone was stripped and led down into the river to be washed. This was not done to make the hunter clean, for Boone was cleaner than the Indians to start with.

It was done, so the Indians said, "to wash away all the white blood."

After this one of the Indians painted Boone's face in an odd red-and-green-and-black design. When he had put on his moccasins and had wrapped a fur robe about his body, he looked like a real Indian.

In the village Boone was watched carefully. The Indians thought he might try to run away. But the prisoner acted cheerful and contented. An old Indian couple took him as their son. Now the Indians were sure he would not try to escape. The white man began to go hunting and fishing with his red "brothers." The Indians liked contests in running, jumping, and shooting at a mark. Boone joined them in these sports, but he was always careful to let some of the best warriors beat him.

The run-away. Daniel Boone looked and acted like an Indian. But he was still a white man. He worried about Boonesboro and about his family. He wanted to go home. Then something happened that told him he must get back to his fort and his people. The Indian village where he lived began filling with warriors who came hurrying in, in single file, along all the forest paths. They had their guns and their tomahawks. They were painted for war. And worst of all, Boone, listening, heard them say that they were going into Kentucky to capture Boonesboro.

The next morning Boone walked carelessly into the

woods. When he was out of sight of the wigwams, he started to run. For three days and nights he ran on and on, stopping to rest only when too tired to take another step. He swam the Ohio River and hurried on to Boonesboro. Imagine the joy of the people in the fort at the sight of their old leader running toward them out of the forest.

When the Indians came down to the fort and tried to capture it, the white men were ready for them and quickly drove them away.

Here are sentences in which words are missing. Can you write them on a sheet of paper, choosing the right missing word from the list below the sentences and writing it where it belongs?

1. Daniel Boone went along a path called the ____ to get to ____.
2. In the new country Boone and his men built a ____.
3. A place where water comes up from the ground is called a ____.
4. When Boone was a ____ of the Indians they made him look like them. So he is called in one of these stories a ____.
5. On their feet the Indians wore ____. In war the Indian carried a ____. An Indian's ____ was the tuft of long hair on the top of his head.

moccasins	spring	Wilderness Road
fort	prisoner	scalp lock
Kentucky	tomahawk	white Indian

VI. HOW OUR NATION, THE UNITED STATES, WAS BEGUN

CHAPTER FOURTEEN. QUARRELS WITH ENGLAND, THE MOTHER COUNTRY

"EVERY MAN'S HOUSE IS HIS CASTLE"

Just before France and England ended their wars over the western and northern lands, a new king came to the throne of England. His title was George III. He was a good young man in many ways, but he wanted to have his own way. He wanted to be a strong king. England, so George III felt, should make the people in America obey the laws of the mother country.

The colonists wanted to manage their own affairs. They had been doing this for a long time, and, now that they were strong, they did not see why they should not go on looking out for themselves. But the king sent some of his officers to America to make the colonists obey some of the old English laws.

The ship owners and their troubles. As you already know, the American merchants owned many ships. These ships sailed in many directions across the seas, carrying goods from the colonial cities to distant ports. When the vessels came home they brought cargoes of goods to be sold in America. The English laws told the American merchants what goods must be taken to England only, and ordered them to buy for use in America only articles sold to them by the merchants of England.

The officers the king sent to America began searching everywhere for goods that had come to the colonies from other countries. They broke open the doors of barns and sheds and looked for the goods that had been brought in, or smuggled. They went into the houses of the people and hunted through them from attic to cellar.

James Otis. In Boston lived a pale, sickly young lawyer by the name of James Otis. He had a position

under the king's government. But when he learned what the king's officers were doing, he gave up his place in order to be free to fight for the rights of the people. He began to make speeches in which he showed how wrong it was for the king's men to break into a house, using the excuse that they were hunting for smuggled goods. He cried that in America "Every man's house is his castle." Can you see what he meant by that?

James Otis' speeches made his listeners even more angry with the mother country and King George III. Many of the colonists began to feel that England was no longer their true friend but had become their enemy.

Why did the men sent to America by King George want to search the houses and other buildings in the colonies?

What is meant by "smuggled" goods? Have you ever heard of any kind of "smuggling" that sometimes goes on now?

How did many of the people in America begin to feel toward the mother country?

SONS AND DAUGHTERS OF LIBERTY

Many years ago some strange things began to happen in Boston, and New York, and the other colonial towns and villages. If we had been living in America then, we should have seen some surprising sights.

Past our house goes the richest man in town. But where are his velvet cloak, his silk stockings, and his rich, plum-colored vest? He is dressed in clothing of

plain, rough cloth, made in our town, and not brought in from England. Has the man lost all his money?

Then we visit one of the big houses of the town. There in a corner of the kitchen sits the mistress of the fine house. And, of all things, she is spinning. Not since the earliest times had anyone in that rich home worked at a spinning wheel. Then we notice the lady's shoes. Where are the soft, dainty ones such as the fine lady always has sent to her from across the seas in Europe? She is wear-

ing coarse, heavy, clumsy shoes, made, as we know at a glance, by one of our own poor village shoemakers. What has happened?

Everywhere it is the same. People seem bent on wearing only the plainest and coarsest things they can find. Then a butcher, to whose shop we go to buy some mutton, gives us a hint.

"I'm sorry, but I can't sell you any mutton. I can't sell mutton to anybody. I promised not to. And nobody but you has asked for mutton. You see, it's this way: if none of us Americans eat mutton, none of the American sheep will have to be killed. If the sheep all live they'll each have a nice wool coat. And with the wool our wives and daughters can make all our clothes. Then we won't have to buy any of these things from England."

After a time we learn all about what has happened. The king's government in England had passed a law taxing the people in the colonies. The law was called the Stamp Act because the people were made to buy English stamps of many kinds. The people in America did not want to pay a tax put on them by the mother country. The men began to meet and form themselves

into groups called the Sons of Liberty. The women took the name, Daughters of Liberty. They made up their minds to one thing: they would get along without goods from England until the Stamp Act was no longer a law. They believed that wearing home-made suits and coarse shoes would not hurt them as much as the English merchants would be harmed by the loss of trade.

Very soon the English merchants and ship owners began to lose money. They could not sell the things they brought to America. When the king and his officers saw this, they gave up the stamp law. So the people in America won this fight against being taxed by England.

Finish these "because" sentences.
1. The people would not eat mutton because ____.
2. The people wore coarse shoes because ____.
3. The English merchants lost money because ____.
4. The king gave up the Stamp Act because ____.

TEA AND SALT WATER

Very soon the people in America had a new quarrel with King George and his government. A new tax law had been passed. This time the tax was on tea.

Of course, the people in the colonies could not raise tea. They had to buy it. The tea came from the East, and was brought to Boston and Charleston and Baltimore and the other towns in the ships of the English merchants. The people in America liked tea. They drank much more tea, and much less coffee, than people do

today. But many of them decided to go without tea rather than to help the king get his tax money.

At Philadelphia a crowd threatened the pilots with a coat of tar and feathers if they brought the tea ships to the wharves. In Charleston the tea was taken off the ships, but was stored in damp places where it spoiled.

One dark night in Boston some of the children were scared very nearly out of their wits. They heard wild yells outside their homes, and, peeping out, saw what they thought to be a great crowd of Indians dashing down the street. The hurrying figures looked like

Indians, too. Their faces were painted. They had
feathers in their hair, and bright blankets wrapped
about their bodies. In their hands were clubs and tomahawks. The yells that rose from the hurrying dark
crowd were enough to scare any one.

But the terrible "Mohawk Indians" were only men
of Boston. They were not looking for a chance to harm
people, but for tea. Of course, they knew where the tea
was. It was on the ships in the harbor. The ships would
not sail away with the tea, and the people of Boston
would not allow the tea to be taken off. Something had
to be done, so the "Mohawk war party" was planned.

The "Indians" took boats and rowed out to the tea ships. They scrambled on board the ships, and a few minutes later three hundred forty-two chests of tea were slowly settling into the waters of Boston Harbor.

The king and his men were very angry about the tea. But of course they could not find any of the "Indians" to punish them. Instead, they got ready to punish the entire town of Boston.

Is it clear to you that the people were not really thinking about tea at all? It was the tax that angered them.

This is a good story to tell. Plan just how you will "put it together": first, the plans of the King's government; next, the arrival of the tea ships; next, the problem about the tea on the ships at Boston; and last, the "tea party."

Can you draw a picture to represent what happened on board the ships?

THE SIGNAL IN THE CHURCH STEEPLE

By this time, you may be sure, King George thought he had some very bad people living in his colonies. After the "tea party" he felt certain that most of them lived at Boston. He sent over more soldiers to watch them.

The Boston people lost their chance to carry on trade. Food in the town became scarce. Some of the people would have gone hungry if people in the other colonies had not sent them great wagon loads of food. The colonists were learning to hate and fear the king's soldiers and were about ready to start a great fight against them.

Dr. Joseph Warren. One night Dr. Joseph Warren, of Boston, heard strange noises on the street near his home. He could hear the tramp of many feet and the sounds of swords and guns clanging against each other. When he went out to see what it was all about, he found the streets full of soldiers.

By listening to the low voices of the captains Dr. Warren learned where the soldiers were going. They were getting ready to march to the little town of Concord to destroy a supply of powder and bullets belonging to the colonists. They were going to try to capture two of the American leaders.

Dr. Warren was a good American. He had thought that perhaps the soldiers would try some such plan as this. He had thought out what he would do to warn the people outside Boston of this secret night march of the soldiers.

Now the town of Boston was on a narrow piece of land. Dr. Warren knew that some of the king's soldiers were standing guard with their guns where the road ran from Boston out into the country. Then how could a person warn the people that the "redcoats" were coming?

Dr. Warren had his plan. Beyond the narrow place he had two men waiting. These two men held the reins

of their fast horses and watched and waited. At last they saw it. The signal! A light in the steeple of the Old North Church, in Boston. It was Dr. Warren's signal telling the watchers that the soldiers were on the march and what way they would go.

Paul Revere and William Dawes. The men waiting with their horses were Paul Revere and William Dawes. They had agreed to be ready to ride and warn the people that the king's soldiers were coming. When they saw the signal in the church steeple they sprang to their horses' backs, wheeled, and galloped away in the darkness. Before morning came, the people for miles around knew that the red-coated soldiers of England were marching on the road toward Concord.

Can you answer these questions?
Who—
    planned the scheme to warn the people?
    rode in the night to warn the people?
Where—
    was the light of warning?
    were the English soldiers marching to?
    did Dr. Warren live?
Why—
    were the English soldiers marching?
    did Dr. Warren want to warn the people?

The Minute Men

In Lexington, a town not far from Boston, stands a statue of a young soldier. The statue is called "The Minute Man." Who were the minute men?

Some of the American leaders were certain the men in the colonies would have to fight for their rights against the soldiers from England. They thought that America should have soldiers, too. So the men and boys in the towns began holding meetings where they drilled and practiced as soldiers. They learned to carry their guns as soldiers carry theirs, and to march together keeping step. They said they would drop whatever they were doing and hurry to any place where they were needed to defend the colonists. So they were called minute men.

The minute men heard the message of Paul Revere and William Dawes. They took their guns and hurried across the fields toward Concord and Lexington. Soon they could see the king's soldiers in their red coats marching down the road.

The soldiers and the minute men fought at Lexington, at Concord, and along the road which led to Boston. Many men on each side were struck down by the

flying bullets. The soldiers of England were glad when they were safe again in Boston. Now at last it was clear that there was going to be a real war between the angry people of America and England, their mother country.

A. Answer these questions:

Why were some of the men living near Boston called minute men?

In this story it is said that the men in the colonies would have to fight for their rights. What do you think some of these rights were?

What is meant when England is spoken of as the "mother country" of the colonists?

B. What happened—

when George III had passed a law called the Stamp Act?

when the colonists refused to buy goods sent from England?

when the king had a tax put on tea?

when the Americans heard about the tax?

when the tea ships arrived at Boston?

when Dr. Warren heard the king's soldiers on the streets?

when the two riders got his signal?

when the soldiers marched to Lexington and Concord?

C. Finish the sentences.

The king of England at this time was ＿＿.

His soldiers were often called ＿＿.

The girls and women who would not buy goods from England were called ＿＿.

The "Mohawk Indians" in one of these stories were really ＿＿.

The leader who sent the message from the church steeple was ＿＿.

His messengers were ＿＿ and ＿＿.

A young man of Boston who said that no one had a right to break into a man's house was ＿＿.

The colonial men who were ready to fight the soldiers were called ＿＿.

CHAPTER FIFTEEN. STORIES OF THE TIMES WHEN WE BECAME A NATION

GEORGE WASHINGTON, LEADER OF THE SOLDIERS

Where was George Washington during all the years when the people of America were drifting into a war with King George III and the mother country, England? All this time he had been living at his Mount Vernon home, in Virginia. He spent much of his time managing his great farm on the banks of the Potomac River. But George Washington remembered that he, too, was an American. He did not at all like the way George III of England was treating the American people.

One spring day in the year 1775, Washington set out on horseback to ride to Philadelphia. Leading men from the colonies were to meet there, and Washington was one of the men sent by Virginia to the Congress. The colonial leaders were going to plan what ought to be done to save the rights of the colonists.

News from Boston. A messenger rode to Philadelphia from Boston with news. He told the men at the Congress about the fight between the minute men and the soldiers at Lexington. Washington and the others saw then that there was to be a war between the colonies and England.

One day the men at Philadelphia voted for a leader for the soldiers America would need in the war. George Washington was chosen. He told the men of Congress that he did not believe himself well prepared to command the soldiers. He said he thought he would make many mistakes. But he promised to do the best he could for America.

The general and his soldiers. So George Washington, who had expected soon to go back to Mount Vernon to care for his plantation, hurried away toward Boston where the soldiers were. It was a long horseback journey for him and his companions.

At Cambridge, near Boston, the American soldiers were drawn up in long lines to receive their new general. There, under a large elm tree, George Washington took command of the men who had gathered to fight the king's soldiers. The elm tree was carefully preserved from that day on. It was called the Cambridge Elm.

Finish the sentences.

George Washington rode from his home at ____ to the meeting at ____. Then he rode on to join the patriot army near ____.

How did Washington feel when he was made commander of the soldiers?

Choose from this list some words that describe Washington.

modest	selfish	afraid
brave	boastful	a good leader
patriotic	brave	

THE LIBERTY BELL

The people of Pennsylvania were proud of a new building that stood on Chestnut Street, in Philadelphia. It was the building where the government of the colony was carried on. It was called the Capitol or State House.

After a time a bell tower rose above the roof of the State House. The tower needed a bell, so the leaders sent to England and had made there a great bell. Stamped into the metal of the bell were the words, "Proclaim liberty throughout all the land to all the inhabitants thereof."

One day in the summer of 1776 the people gathered outside the State House were all talking at once. A meeting was going on inside the State House. The men in the meeting were voting. Their vote would decide whether America was to try to free itself from England and form a new nation. Do you wonder that the waiting crowd was talking so much?

At last the great news reached the people outside. The men had voted in favor of the Declaration of Independence. That meant that America was to become a free nation. A few days later the famous Declaration was read to the people of Philadelphia. The great bell on the State House rang joyfully.

The events of July 4, 1776, changed some names on Chestnut Street, Philadelphia. The State House became Independence Hall. The State House Yard became Independence Square. The bell became the Liberty Bell.

What day is called the birthday of our country?

Why can Independence Hall be called the birthplace of our country?

A New Flag for a New Nation

When the soldiers of the colonies gathered to fight against the armies of England, they wanted to have a flag. They knew they would march better if they could see a flag waving above them. If they had a flag to defend, they thought they would fight more bravely.

But at first the soldiers had no single flag to honor. They had many flags. The soldiers from the different colonies often brought with them flags that had been made for them before they left home. One flag the soldiers liked showed a picture of a coiled snake. Below the snake were the words, "Don't tread on me."

One of the American ship captains sailed away on his ship, the "Ranger," to fight the English ships. The captain's name was John Paul Jones. The flag floating above his ship had stripes to represent the colonies. There were stars on the flag. It had been made by the girls of Portsmouth, New Hampshire, and given to John Paul Jones for his ship. It is said that the white part of the flag was made from a wedding dress.

When George Washington joined the soldiers near Boston he had a flag with seven red and six white stripes in it. Each stripe, of course, stood for one of the thirteen colonies. But in the corner of Washington's flag were the crosses used in the flag of England. The crosses showed that the people of the colonies still felt that America belonged to England.

But what happened the next year, on July 4, 1776, changed all that. Can you see why? Now a flag was needed for a new nation. It is said that Betsey Ross, of Philadelphia, with the help of other women, helped Washington plan the first truly American flag. It was like our flag today—except that on the blue field in the corner there were only thirteen stars and the stars were arranged in a circle. Perhaps you can explain why the stars are no longer in a circle on our flag.

On June 14, 1777, Congress voted for the flag Washington had helped plan. Ever since that time June 14 has been known as Flag Day.

How many stars were in the first flag of our country?
How many are there now?
Has the number of stripes increased? Why not? How many are there?
What is meant by Flag Day? When is it?

Washington and his soldiers fought on, year after year, against the armies sent by King George to America. Sometimes they won battles. Often they were beaten by the soldiers of England. Washington was brave and patient through all his troubles.

One early winter day Washington led his ragged army into the hills of Pennsylvania. Some of the soldiers marched barefoot. The snow and ice cut their feet so that they left blood on the snow where they had stepped.

The place where the soldiers ended their march was called Valley Forge. There Washington and his men got ready to spend the long, cold winter. The leader divided his soldiers into groups of twelve. He told each group of men to build a log cabin for themselves. He offered a prize to the men who first finished their small house. Soon the hillsides at Valley Forge were dotted with the cabins of the soldiers.

At Valley Forge there was very little food for the soldiers. The snow got deep, and the hungry soldiers found it hard to keep warm. Some of the men became sick and died. At one time three thousand of the men had so little to wear that they could not be called on to go outside and help guard the camp. Every now and then a soldier left and crept away to his distant home.

But the good soldiers stayed with Washington. They

laughed at their troubles and at the idea of giving up.
Washington and his officers made a joke of their own
poor food and ragged clothing. One night some of the
officers gave a party for the others. No one could come
to the party unless he could show a hole worn through
his clothing.

The soldiers spent many cold winters in the armies of
the new American nation. But Valley Forge was the
worst, because the men were almost without hope. After

that hard winter many of them began to see, as Washington did, that if they were brave they might win the war and make America free.

Try to find a picture of one of Washington's soldiers. Notice his hat, coat, breeches, stockings, and shoes.

Tell a story about the hardships of the soldiers at Valley Forge.

From this list choose the reasons why the winter at Valley Forge was a hard one.

1. The soldiers did not have enough clothes to keep them warm.
2. The snow was deep.
3. There was little food.
4. The men did not like Washington.
5. Many were sick.
6. Many were barefooted.
7. They lived in tents.

When Nathan Hale was a college boy at Yale College he was loved and respected by the other students. He was a good student and good at games, as well. He broke the college record for jumping. When he finished college he began teaching school. One day the news reached his school that war between the colonists and the soldiers had begun near Boston. Nathan forgot all about his school. The next day he was marching north with other soldiers on his way to Boston.

The spy. In the second year of the war Washington and his soldiers were in trouble. They had pushed the redcoats out of Boston, but now the soldiers of King George had forced them out of New York. Washington was worried. He did not know just where all his enemies were, or how many there were, or what they planned to do next. At last he sent this word to one of his officers:

"Gather your captains and other officers in one place. Tell them we must find out what our enemies are doing, and what plans they are making. Then call for a volunteer to go as a spy into the camps of the English soldiers and learn what we must know."

None of the officers wanted to be a spy. It was one thing to die bravely fighting on the field of battle, and quite another to be caught as a spy and hanged. Not a man stepped forward and offered to go on the dangerous journey for Washington. Then Nathan Hale, now a

captain, entered the room. When he heard what Washington wanted he said quietly, "I will go."

A few days later a young man dressed in a brown suit and wearing a broad-rimmed hat tramped up to where some of the English soldiers were standing guard. He told them that he was a school teacher, and that he did not want to serve in the army of Washington. He showed the soldiers his papers from Yale College. The men of the guard could see no harm in letting the school teacher go past them and on into the city of New York where the main army of the king's men was camped. The young man was Nathan Hale.

Captured by the English soldiers. Washington's spy wandered about joking with the English soldiers and listening keenly to all that was said. Very soon he had learned the things Washington so badly needed to know. Each night, in a small room, he carefully set down on thin strips of paper all that he had learned.

A boat was to come to a place called The Cedars, take Nathan Hale on board, and carry him back to the army. The spy reached The Cedars before it was time for the boat. He decided to wait in a nearby tavern, or hotel. In the tavern he visited with a few red-coated soldiers who happened to be there. Nathan Hale did not notice that a man in the tavern looked at him sharply and then slipped outside.

After a while a man came into the tavern and said that a strange boat was coming towards the shore. Nathan Hale said good-bye to his companions and walked down to the dock. He was sure the boat had come for him. He was happy to think that he would soon be with Washington, telling his general all that he had learned.

Poor Nathan Hale! The men in the boat were his enemies, waiting for him. They raised their guns and ordered him to surrender. When they searched him they found his notes under a loose sole in one of his shoes.

Nathan Hale was to die early the next morning. He had been caught as a spy. He spent his last hours writing letters to his loved ones. When he was marched out to be hanged he saw the English officer tear up all the letters he had written.

In the city of New York stands a beautiful statue to the memory of the hero, Nathan Hale. On it are carved his last words, "I regret that I have but one life to give for my country."

A. Can you answer these questions?

Why did Washington want one of his men to go into the camp of the English soldiers?

How did Nathan Hale get past the guard of soldiers and into New York?

How did the English find out that Nathan Hale was a spy?

B. Match these.

1. a spy   a. to give up to the enemy
2. a volunteer   b. one who does a brave deed
3. a hero   c. one who freely offers to help
4. to surrender d. one who learns the secrets of an enemy in order to help his own country

WILLIAM JASPER AND THE FLAG

The captains of England's war ships decided to try
to capture the city of Charleston, South Carolina. They
thought that would be a good way to cause the colonists
to lose the war. Soon ten great ships of war entered
Charleston harbor.

On a low island in the harbor stood a new log fort.
In the fort were the colonial soldiers. They had a number of long, heavy cannons, but they did not have much
powder to load them with. How could one log fort drive

away the ships of England? The people of Charleston feared that their fort and all the men in it would be battered to pieces.

The great guns roared for many hours. Heavy cannon balls crashed into the sides of the fort. But the logs of the fort were of a soft wood. Between the double wall of logs there was sand. The shots from the ships did not damage the fort. But the cannon balls from the fort broke down the masts of the ships and smashed holes in their sides. The ships lost the battle and sailed away. After that the people of Charleston gave their fort a new name. They named it Fort Moultrie, after Colonel Moultrie, who had built it and had saved their city from the enemy.

A young Irish lad was one of the soldiers at Fort Moultrie. His name was William Jasper. All at once, in the thickest of the fight, he noticed that the "rattlesnake" flag which had waved above the fort was down. That would never do! William Jasper crept outside, picked up the flag, fastened it once more to its staff, and put the staff back in place. All this time the bullets were whistling past him. But the brave Irish boy got back inside the fort without being hurt.

Jasper fought on in the army for three years more. At last he found himself helping to defend another fort. This fort stood in the harbor of Savannah, Georgia. Then the strangest thing happened. Just as at Fort Moultrie, the flag above the fort was shot down. And just as at Fort Moultrie the Irish boy went out for it. He reached the flag and gathered it in his arms. Then a bullet struck him and he fell dead, with the flag still in his arms.

The people of Charleston wanted the children, all down through the years, to remember about William Jasper. They built a fine statue in his memory. The figure has one hand stretched toward the island where Fort Moultrie stood. The other hand holds an American flag.

What do these words mean?

   cannon   "rattlesnake" flag

Why did the people want to erect a monument to the memory of William Jasper?

What words would you place on the monument?

The Swamp Fox

The war to make our country free dragged on for a number of years. The king sent his soldiers into South Carolina and Georgia, far in the South. The soldiers took some of the cities and beat some of the armies the colonists sent against them.

But in the South there were leaders who would not stop fighting. Even though they and their men were too few to fight real battles against the king's soldiers, they did all they could to keep the redcoats from going where they pleased. The most daring of these southern leaders was Francis Marion.

Fighting like Indians. Marion had only a few men with him. They had to be very careful not to fall into the hands of the English soldiers. They crept through the woods as silently as so many Indians. The hiding place of the "Swamp Fox" and his men was an island far away in the swamp. For food they had only hominy, rice, and sweet potatoes. They used strips of bark for plates. The first swords the men had were made from saws. Metal mugs and silver plates were melted at fires and then hammered into molds for making lead bullets.

The "Fox" at his tricks. One time a great band of English soldiers was marching along a road which led down to the sea coast. They were hurrying because they had with them as prisoners one hundred fifty soldiers. One of Marion's sharp-eyed scouts saw the English and hurried to the island hiding place with the news.

At once the "Swamp Fox" and his men hurried away through the wet country. They took boats and crossed a deep river to where they had left their horses. A few minutes later they galloped away through the forest.

Late that night the roar of guns all around their camp waked the English soldiers. Marion's men had crept up close in the darkness. Then, yelling and firing their guns, they swept toward the camp. The surprised English soldiers fled in all directions. All their prisoners suddenly found themselves free again.

The soldiers of the king grew tired of trying to catch Marion. They were glad when at last they could march away out of reach of the "Swamp Fox."

Why was Marion called the "Swamp Fox"?

The book says his men "fought like Indians." What does that mean?

Find out what hominy is.

"I Have Just Begun to Fight"

John Paul Jones was born so near the ocean that the roaring of the great waves could be heard in his home. When he was still only a boy he owned a little sailboat. One day the captain of a ship saw John Paul sail his boat into the harbor. The boy showed himself to be such a

good little sailor that the captain gave him the post of
cabin boy on his ship. On this ship John Paul made his
first voyage across the ocean from his home in Scotland
to America.

Not so many years passed before the lad from Scotland was Captain John Paul Jones and had his own
ship. In the war to make America free he was on the side
of the colonists. He went out to sea to fight the English
in a fine, new ship called the "Ranger." An earlier
story told how the girls of Portsmouth gave him a flag
for his ship.

A famous sea battle. After a time Captain Jones had command of another ship, the "Bonhomme Richard." It was an old vessel and not very strong. But in it the brave captain began a battle with one of England's fine ships. The cannons on the two ships kept up a steady roar. The masts were broken, and the sails hung in rags above the decks. Many of the men on the "Bonhomme Richard" lay about the deck dead or dying. The two vessels crashed together, and with his own hands the American captain lashed them together. By this time the American ship had so many cannon-ball holes in its sides that it was beginning to sink. The English captain shouted:

"Do you surrender?"

"Surrender? I've just begun to fight!" John Paul Jones roared back at him.

It was true. The Americans shot so straight and fast that the English sailors dared not stay on the deck of their ship. Their cannons were silent. At last the English captain surrendered his ship to John Paul Jones. Captain Jones and his men quickly gathered up the wounded American sailors and moved them to the deck of the captured ship.

The end of the "Bonhomme Richard." The old "Bonhomme Richard" sank lower and lower in the water. Then it disappeared under the waves. The last thing to be seen as the ship sank was the flag that the girls had given to John Paul Jones. He could have saved his flag. But he thought it would be wrong to his dead sailors who were going down into the sea with the "Bonhomme Richard."

Find a picture of a fighting ship in the days of John Paul Jones. Notice the tall masts and the wide spread of its many sails.

Finish these sentences.

1. The boyhood home of John Paul Jones was in ____.
2. He sailed away to fight for America in a ship called ____.
3. In his most famous sea fight Captain Jones commanded the ship ____.
4. The English captain asked Jones, "____?"
5. John Paul Jones answered, "____."
   Why did John Paul Jones leave his flag on the sinking "Bonhomme Richard"?

THE MAN WITH TWO COUNTRIES

Lafayette was a rich young Frenchman. One time at a dinner he heard an Englishman telling about the war going on in America. Lafayette listened, and all at once decided that he wanted to help the Americans.

But England and France were at peace, so the king of France would not let Lafayette sail away to America to fight against England. He told him to stay where he was. The eager young Frenchman disobeyed his king, bought a ship of his own, and crossed the ocean to help George Washington in the war.

Washington and Lafayette. George Washington liked the young French lad. He soon found that Lafayette was a good soldier. The two became warm friends. Lafayette at last helped his general to capture one of the English armies and win freedom for America.

America's friend. When the war was over Lafayette went back to France, and George Washington went to

his Mount Vernon home. Three years after this Lafayette came back to America for a visit. Everywhere he went he was honored as one of the heroes of the war. He traveled about and visited the places where he had fought for the Americans. But he spent as much time as he could with his old friend at Mount Vernon.

The next time Lafayette visited our country he was an old, old man. His friend, George Washington, was dead. But the people of America had not forgotten Lafayette. They heaped honors upon him. They were grateful to him for what he had done for America. But he was grateful to America, too. He had lost his fortune, but people in America had sent him money and had given him land in Louisiana. They treated their good friend of earlier times almost as if he were truly a citizen of our country.

It can be said, then, that the French hero, Lafayette,

has two countries: his native country, France, and the United States.

Why did the king of France tell Lafayette that he could not go to America?

In what ways did the people of America show that they liked Lafayette and wanted to honor him?

What are some of the ways by which visitors to our country are honored? Make a list of all you can think of.

Match the names of persons with the sentences that go with them.

1. Paul Revere   a. This Frenchman helped America.
2. Lafayette   b. He was a famous sea fighter.
3. George III   c. He rode to warn the colonists.
4. Joseph Warren   d. He was a soldier who was always ready.
5. Nathan Hale   e. She helped make our flag.
6. minute man   f. He was a ruler who wanted to punish his subjects.
7. Betsey Ross   g. He gave a signal from a church steeple.
8. William Jasper   h. He replaced the flag after it had been shot down.
9. Francis Marion   i. He was a patriot spy.
10. John Paul Jones   j. He did a great deal for America with just a few soldiers.

There are nine stories in this long chapter. Which one do you like best? Why? Practice telling it, and then tell it before your classmates.

CHAPTER SIXTEEN. PLANNING A
BETTER AMERICA

A GREAT NEW NATION

After George Washington and his soldiers had won the long war, America was free. The thirteen colonies that had once belonged to England now became the United States. The United States, our country, is now more than one hundred fifty years old. That may seem quite old to you. But, after all, many other countries are much older than that.

Our new nation was very large, even at first. It was much larger than most of the countries in Europe. In the west it reached all the way to the Mississippi River. In this new United States there were millions and mil-

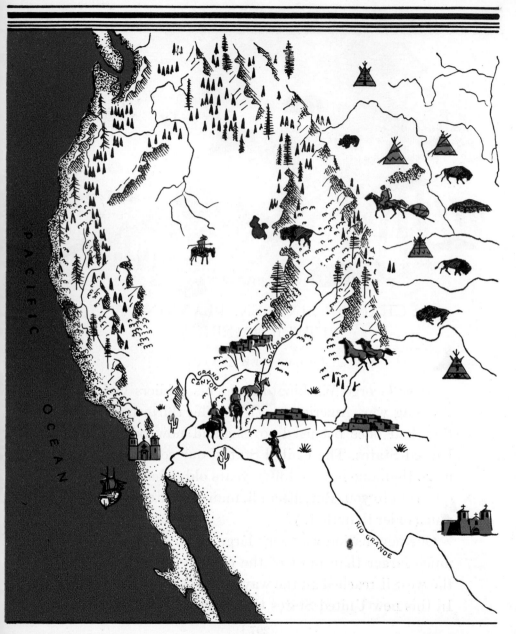

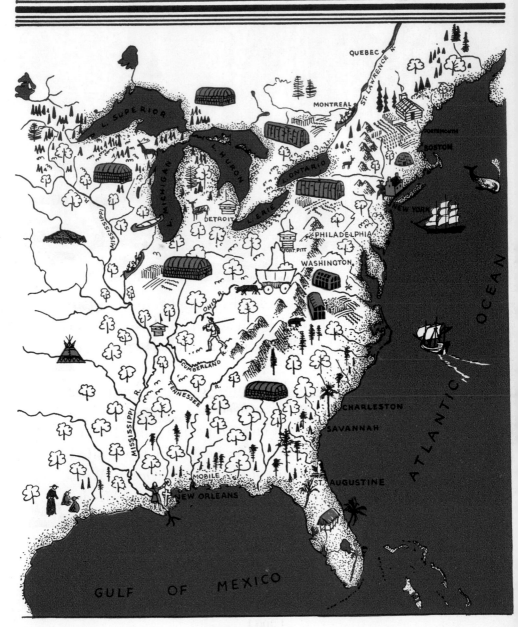

lions of acres of rich farm lands. Grand forests of oak trees, and of maple and birch and pine trees, spread widely across the land. In the ground were rich stores of iron and coal and oil.

But most of the lands and most of the riches of our new America were not being used in George Washington's time. There were not enough people living here to use them. Almost all the white people in the United States lived near the shores of the Atlantic Ocean. West of where these people were, all the way to the Mississippi River, lived the Indians. The red people, of course, did not make much use of the rich soil and the fine timber all about them. Around the villages of the Indians roamed wild animals in numbers almost as great as in the very earliest times.

A great part of our new United States was still waiting for the people who could make good use of its riches. Think of such great cities as Chicago, Cleveland, Cincinnati, and Atlanta. When the United States began, only the wild animals and the Indians lived in the forests which then grew where these cities stand today.

In what way was the new United States large, even at first?

In what way was it a small nation?

MAKING READY FOR PIONEER FARMERS

What was our new country to do with all the wild, empty land it owned? The leaders decided it would be wise to get settlers to go to these lands and there make their homes.

One of the first things that was done was to divide the western land into squares, and then divide the squares into still smaller pieces of land. Each piece of land, large and small, was given a number different from that of every other piece. This would help the farmer to choose the piece of land he wanted.

The price of the new land was very low. When the poor people in the older settlements heard about the good land, and how cheap it was, many of them got ready to move to the West. They were promised that when enough of them had gone to one of these western divisions that part of the country would be made into a state in the United States. The trip to the West was a long, hard journey in those days. But very soon white people were making their homes in what are now the states of Ohio, Indiana, and Illinois.

In Chapter Thirteen you learned about Daniel Boone and James Robertson and the forts they and their friends began in Kentucky and Tennessee. They went into the wild lands to live even before it was decided that there was to be any United States at all. They were happy when they learned that their new little towns, and all the forest around them, were a part of the new nation. Hundreds of families hurried over the mountain trails to join the first settlers in Kentucky and Tennessee. Kentucky was the first truly pioneer state in the United States, and Tennessee was the second.

What do you think the word "pioneer" means?

Find on a map the five states mentioned in this story.

What river separates Kentucky from the states of Ohio, Indiana, and Illinois?

Pick out from the list the things a farmer would look for when he chose lands for a new farm home out in the western country.

1. a place where there were no trees
2. a heavy forest
3. the ground covered with large rocks
4. many high hills
5. a river or creek running through the land
6. a place where there were groves of good trees and also openings where there were few trees

A New Government for a New Nation

What boy or girl does not know that Washington, in the District of Columbia, is our *capital* city? Look at the picture on this page. Could you name the building in the picture if you saw it somewhere else than in a history book? Of course you could. You knew at once that it was the *capitol* of our country.

Would it seem odd to live in our United States and know that it had no true capital city and no capitol building at all? And no president and no White House for the president to live in? Our new country, after the colonies had won their freedom from England, had none of these things.

Of course the new nation had a government. For a time the meetings of the government officers took place in New York City. The buildings used for the government were borrowed or rented buildings. Our government owned no buildings at first. A number of years passed before the first government buildings were built in the new capital city of Washington.

Only a few men, in those early times, spent their time doing the business of the government. Not many were needed, because the government was quite simple. Most of the men were in a Congress. They all met together in one group and made the laws. This Congress did not have much power to rule the people. It could not collect taxes from the people. The taxes were gathered by the states. Congress could not even settle the troubles the states had with each other. Such things as helping the farmers, or fighting forest fires, or sending out weather reports, or helping catch kidnapers had not even been dreamed of as work that the government should do.

Perhaps by this time you will begin to think that the first government of the United States was little better than no government at all. George Washington and other men of that time began to think very much the same thing.

When you write about Washington, our capital city, be sure to spell capital with a *tal.* If you are writing about our main government building write capitol with a *tol.*

How many of you have been at Washington? Tell the class what you saw there.

A Fresh Start

George Washington said, "We are one today and thirteen tomorrow." He meant, of course, that the thirteen states might not stay together to form a nation. He feared they would separate and that there would be no United States at all.

At last many of the people in America saw that if they were to have a real nation they must have a better government. Fifty-five of the leading men from the different states started on the long journey to Philadelphia. In that city they planned to hold a meeting to see what could be done about the government. Most of them traveled on horseback along the muddy roads, stopping to rest and sleep each night at some inn. One by one they came at last to Philadelphia.

One day a man rode into the city from the south. The others were glad when this man arrived. With him there, they thought their meeting would be a success. You know who this man was, do you not? Yes, it was George Washington. Nothing very important happened in our new country in those days that Washington did not have a hand in.

The men at Philadelphia gathered in Independence Hall for their meeting. That was the place, you remember, where the Declaration of Independence was made. One of the men at the meeting was wise, friendly Benjamin Franklin, then a very old man. George Washington was chosen to be the leader. Soon the men were all hard at work at the task of making the good plan of government we Americans have today.

Benjamin Franklin had a long and interesting and helpful life. Three stories in this book have told about him. It would be interesting to read these stories again and then plan to write a short story about Franklin. You could begin by telling about his boyhood, and how he became a printer. What would come next in your story? And after that?

Why did the men at Philadelphia feel that they needed Washington there to make the meeting a success?

Why was this meeting held?

What important thing was done at the meeting?

CHAPTER SEVENTEEN. LOOKING TOWARD THE FUTURE

How Our New Nation Grew in Size

When our new nation, the United States of America, first started, it reached to the west as far as the Mississippi River. That made of it a pretty big country—much larger than many of the famous European countries. And, as you know, very few white people were living in all its western parts. It did not seem as though the United States needed to be any larger.

But we had hardly got started as a nation when we began to grow in size. There was a reason, which you will learn about in your next history book, why our country needed to own both banks of the Mississippi River—not just the east bank. So our government bought a great piece of land west of the Father of Waters. This new land almost doubled the size of the United States. There were French people and Spanish people living here and there in the new land. They now became citizens of our country.

Then there was Florida. We did not own Florida at first. It belonged to Spain. Soon we arranged with Spain to buy Florida from her. That was a good thing, for, as you can see by looking at a map, Florida seems a natural part of our country.

Some of our restless people traveled a long trail which led them almost to the Pacific Ocean. The land they went to we now call Oregon and Washington. Of course these people wanted to be in the United States. But England, too, laid claim to all that far country. England and the United States decided not to fight about it. Instead, they ran a line across the mountains and forests dividing the wild western country between the two nations. England took what lay north of the line, while we were to own the lands south of it. England's part, just to the north, is now called British Columbia.

Our country began having trouble with Mexico, the new nation south of us. When Texas left Mexico and joined the United States, the rulers of Mexico did not like it. There was a war, and at its end we added to the United States California, on the shore of the Pacific Ocean, and all the lands between California and what was already ours. A few years later a small strip of territory in the southern parts of what are now the states of Arizona and New Mexico was bought from Mexico.

All this made the United States look just as it looks today. We now reached from the Atlantic Ocean to the Pacific Ocean. Our country was several times larger than it had been at first. It was also many times richer in soil, timber, iron, coal, oil, and precious metals. In fact, it had now become one of the largest and richest countries in the entire world.

The pioneers we talk about here were the people who moved west, and kept moving west, as fast as our country grew in that direction. They saw the different parts of our country just as they were in the old Indian days. They kept learning new things about the trees of America. We have room to speak of only a few of the things they learned.

The pioneers were used to living in the woods. The eastern part of the country was covered with forests. And that, as you know, is where the first American pioneers settled. There were such trees as cypress and palmetto in the south. There were fine oaks and maples and elms scattered about everywhere. All these trees lost their leaves when the frosts came in the fall. Then, too, on the hillsides, in the mountains, and far in the north there were evergreens such as the pines and the cedars. The settlers made good use of the fine, straight trees they found all around them. They built their first houses and barns with some of the logs. They made boards and shingles and posts for their fences from the timber in some of the trees. Sometimes they made furniture, boats, sleds, and wagons out of the trees growing near by.

When the first white men went near the Great Lakes, they found a forest of pine greater than any they had ever seen before. Then, south of there, in Illinois and in other states, they found something that surprised them. They found places where there were no trees at all, but just waving grass. Had some one been there and cut down the trees? No, there had never been any—or not for hundreds of years, anyway. The pioneers had come to the prairies, as such open places are called. Later on, still farther west, they found, not just small prairies, but prairies on all sides of them, as far as they could look. There were almost no trees anywhere. Later on you will learn how the people learned to live in the treeless prairies.

When some of the pioneers got to the west side of the great prairies and the high, windy plains, they saw gleaming mountains before them. Do you know what mountains these were? Yes, the Rocky Mountains. The lower slopes of the mountains were often green with evergreen trees. Not far beyond the mountains, here and there, were petrified forests, forests of stone. The trees of long ago had all died. As the wood in the trees decayed, minerals took the place of the fibres of the wood. When the wood had all rotted away, there were the tree trunks, looking very much as they had in the first place. Only now they were stone and not wood. Have you ever seen a piece of petrified wood?

Out near the shores of the Pacific Ocean the white men found trees larger than any they had ever seen before. In Oregon there were great, shaggy fir trees. In

California the settlers gazed in wonder at the sequoia trees. It is said that some of the sequoias are the oldest living things on our earth. What grand trees they are, and what is being done to preserve them for long years to come, will be told in a book you may study next year.

What New Things the Pioneers Learned about Wild Animals

Our growing country once had a large population of wild animals. But when we say an animal is wild, that does not mean that it is dangerous. Indeed, there were very few animals that would hurt a human being. A few would do it, especially when the human being had surprised them in the woods, or had hurt them. Even most bears are quite harmless and will run away from you far faster than you can run away from them. The great shaggy grizzly bear, though, was often quite quarrelsome. He was, perhaps, the one really dangerous animal in the wild country. Perhaps you are thinking about the wolves. But even the wolves had to be pretty hungry before they would venture to attack a man. People have usually been more scared of wild animals than they should have been. Often the pioneers killed birds and animals that were almost the best friends they had.

The meat of many animals helped the pioneers to make a living at first. The fur of others they sold for the money to buy many of the things they needed.

New Things the Pioneers Learned
about the Indians

Some of the first chapters in this book told you a great deal about the Indians. But the pioneers did not learn all these things about the red men at first. They learned only about the Indians near the Atlantic Ocean. As some of them moved farther toward the west, they began to find new and different tribes of Indians. They found some who lived in round-topped wigwams and others who lived in pointed tepees. Some of the Indians built birch canoes, some had dugouts, and still others had no boats at all. In the deep woods the white men found Indians who made all of their living fishing and hunting. In some places the red people had good fields of corn, beans, squashes, and tobacco.

Out on the open plains they found Indians who spent most of their time on the backs of their swift horses. Many of these Indians followed the great buffalo herds and lived on the flesh of the animals they killed. When the pioneers found their way out to Oregon, they discovered Indians who spent most of their time fishing along the great rivers. Not many of these Indians cared about fighting.

In the desert country the white people first learned about the cliff-dwelling Indians. These Indians often had fields of corn. They were skilled at making baskets and pottery. Near these tribes were others who were very backward. They wandered about searching for small animals they could kill. But in the desert not many of these were to be had. These poor desert Indians learned to eat almost anything they could lay their hands on.

So you see that the Indians were not very much alike in the different parts of this big country. In some ways they did not even look alike. In some tribes most of the people were tall and very straight, while in others many were short and "squatty." But in important ways they were all alike. They had black eyes, high cheek bones, and coarse, straight black hair. While they were not exactly copper colored, they were all of a reddish brown color.

Helping Mother Nature

As the American people moved out across their big country, they learned to love its flashing lakes, wide rivers, deep valleys, and gleaming mountains. Here and there they found strange things such as great natural bridges, roaring waterfalls, caves, geysers, and glaciers. After a long time it was seen to be worth while to keep the beauties and the wonders of the land just as they were. Other people in the years to come would be glad to visit all these places.

At last the Congress of the United States took steps to preserve the most interesting of them. The first thing Congress did was to make a great park out of the place in Wyoming where all the geysers send up their clouds of hot water and steam. This park they named Yellowstone National Park. Then, one at a time, they made other parks until today there are twenty-five of them.

We can pretend, now, that we have just met a forest ranger away out in one of the national forests. This forest is in Idaho, we will say.

"Yes," he says, in answer to our questions, "I'm a government forest ranger. What do I do? Well, I watch the forests. No, I am not exactly afraid that some one will steal them. My biggest job is to see that they do not burn up."

"Will the forests burn? And how would they catch fire?" we ask.

"Most of the trees in the national forests are pine trees and other trees that also have cones on them. Will they burn? Nothing makes a hotter fire than a blazing forest. And a forest fire travels very fast and is hard to put out. Lightning causes some of the fires we have to fight, but careless campers who do not put out their fires cause more of them.

"Am I the only ranger in this national forest? Oh, no. There are dozens of us. We have log camps away up in the hills. We have trails running all through the forest. Men in high lookout stations watch the forest through their strong field glasses. They can telephone to the other rangers when they see smoke or fire in the woods. Then we get there in a hurry and begin our battle to stop the spread of the forest fire. There are many of these forests, millions of acres of them. In each of them are forest rangers like myself."

"Has our country always had forest rangers to guard its forests?" some one asks.

"Well, no. Nobody thought much about the forests in early times, except to cut them down and get rid of them. Our Uncle Sam kept selling or giving away his forests as fast as he could. But one time, not so very long ago, he decided that this was all wrong. 'Why not save the best of the woods, so that the people will always have a supply of good timber and will always have a fine place to go camping and fishing?' Uncle Sam must have thought. Well, that's the way it all began. And that's how it happens that we have national forests and forest rangers today," our new friend finishes with a smile.

This chapter is called "Looking Toward the Future." We have been talking mostly about things that happened between the time we became a nation and now. Does it not seem to you, now that we have taken this brief glimpse into the future, that our people were really just setting out on the most wonderful part of their adventure in the task of making a strong nation and a good nation, here in America? Will you be glad to go on with the adventure in another book?

INDEX

[319]

[322]

Santa Fe, 60, 62
Savannah, 110, 209, 286
scalp lock, 251
schools, 113–117, 119, 173
sequoia, 313
Serra, Father, 63–65
servants, 152–154
"Seven Cities of Gold," 52–54
sheep, 226, 260
ships and shipping, 144–145, 162, 255
shops, 148
Smith, Captain John, 75–76
"Sons of Liberty," 261
South America, 47
South Carolina, 104–107, 232, 287
Spain, 8, 10, 11, 12, 162
Spanish people, 47, 53, 54, 60
spinning and weaving, 225–226, 258
spinning wheel, 128
Spotswood, Governor, 159–161
Squanto, 85, 87, 169
stage coach, 217, 218
Stamp Act, 260, 261
Standish, Miles, 82–83, 86
stockade, 239
Stuyvesant, Peter, 170–172
Superior, Lake, 21, 183
Swamp Fox, 287

taxes, 261, 306
tea, 261
Tennessee, 250, 303
Tennessee River, 242, 243, 244
tepees, 22
Texas, 310
tobacco, 78, 104–106, 137, 149, 232
trade and traders, 7, 94, 146–151,
162–163, 190–191, 194–197,
231, 232, 255–256
trails, 17–19
travel, 7, 11, 24–27, 141–144, 217–219
travois, 27
Turks, 7

United States, 297–301, 305–308

Valley Forge, 278–280
Vespucius, Americus, 11, 12
Vikings, 1, 3, 4
Vinland, 3–4, 11
Virginia, 64, 72, 78, 117–119, 159–161, 173, 199, 200, 202, 232, 271

wampum, 220
Warren, Doctor Joseph, 265
warriors, 34, 35, 37, 38
Washington, city, 18, 305
Washington, George, 151, 173–176, 202–204, 271, 272, 278–280, 281–283, 294–296, 297, 306, 307
West Indies, 50, 132
whales and whalers, 132–133
whipping post, 233
White, John, 19–20, 70–72
White House, 305
wigwam, 19, 21
wilderness road, 239, 240
Williams, Roger, 88–90
Winthrop, John, 88, 144, 145
Wolfe, General, 211, 212
Wyoming, 316

Yale College, 281
Yellowstone Park, 316